# After Much Discussion

# After Much Discussion

A study book which uses the gospels to discover what Christians were discussing in the early days of the Church and invites a response from contemporary authors and groups.

Donald Hilton

Other books by Donald Hilton

Boy into Man
Girl into Woman
Fresh Voices
Prayers for the Church Community
*(in collaboration with Roy Chapman)*
Celebrating Series
Six Men and a Pulpit
A Word in Season
Risks of Faith
Raw Materials of Faith
Results of Faith

Cover Picture by Don King

*Published by:*
National Christian Education Council
Robert Denholm House
Nutfield
Redhill RH1 4HW

*British Library Cataloguing-in-Publication Data:*
Hilton, Donald, 1932
  After much discussion
  1. Bible - Critical studies
  I. Title
  220.6

ISBN 0-7197-0643-2

First Published 1989
Typeset by Birchwood Photosetting Ltd., Tunbridge Wells, Kent.
Printed & bound by The Whitefriars Press Ltd., Tonbridge, Kent.

# Contents

# Acknowledgements

The editor and publishers gratefully acknowledge permission to reproduce the following copyright material:

British Council of Churches:

From *Child in the Church Report*.

Percy Dearmer:

From *Oxford Book of Carols*. Reproduced by permission of Oxford University Press.

C.H.Dodd:

From *The Founder of Christianity*. © 1970. Reproduced by permission of William Collins Sons & Co.

Charles Elliott:

From *Praying the Kingdom*. © 1985. Reproduced by permission of Darton, Longman & Todd Ltd.

John Foster:

From *What are the Churches Doing*. Reproduced by permission of The Religious & Moral Education Press.

Anthony and Richard Hanson:

From *Reasonable Belief*. © 1981. Reproduced by permission of Oxford University Press.

A.E.Harvey:

From *Companion to the New Testament*. © 1970. Reproduced by permission of Cambridge University Press. *Believing and Belonging*. © 1984. Reproduced by permission of S.P.C.K.

Dr Elizabeth Kubler-Ross:

From a broadcast talk published 29 September 1983. Reproduced by permission of *The Listener*.

Fr. Harry Williams:

From *True Resurrection*. Reproduced by permission of Mitchell Beazley Sons & Co. *True Wilderness*. © 1965. Reproduced by permission of Constable & Co Ltd

Biblical verses are from the *New English Bible* © 1970 and are used by permission of Oxford and Cambridge University Presses.

While every effort has been made to secure permission, we may have failed in a few cases to trace or contact the copyright holder. We apologise for any apparent negligence.

For Princes Street United Reformed Church, Norwich, whose members sustained me over sixteen years.

# Introduction

This book began its life when I was invited to lead the Bible Study with which each morning's session of the General Assembly of the United Reformed Church begins. The studies were extended following an invitation by the Cambridge University Extra-Mural Department to give a series of four lectures at the Norwich Christian Centre.

They are now offered to personal readers and to local church study groups in the hope that they will help those who use the book both to understand more about the early Church and the matters which engaged its attention; and also to see how the questions that created discussion amongst the first Christians are still relevant and demand a response in the twentieth century.

The title of the book is derived from the account in Acts 15 of the Jerusalem Council which met to consider one of the most vexing questions the early Church had to resolve: whether Gentiles could be admitted into the Church. The issue was resolved only 'after much discussion'.

I am grateful to those members of the General Assembly who suggested that the Bible Studies should be made available to a wider readership and also to Princes Street United Reformed Church, Norwich where I was then serving as minister. In sharing some of this material as a series of sermons the members of Princes St once again showed their willingness to allow their minister to think aloud and thus assist in an exploration of the Bible.

Leeds 1989                                     Donald Hilton

# How to use this book

Eight sections are coupled in four chapters. In the first section of each chapter we listen in on a discussion in the early Church and note how their debate influenced the way the gospel writers wrote up their story. Then, in the second section of each chapter, we take up the subject the first Christians have given us and share in the debate as contemporary Christians. For example, the first section of Chapter One explores the story of the epileptic boy and how the disciples of Jesus coped with their failure to heal the child. This leads us in the second section to join with some present-day authors in a debate about Christian success and failure in our own time.

The first section of each chapter is subtitled: *The gospel story* and is an exegesis of the Bible passage.

The second section is subtitled: *The wider debate* and, calling on other authors, invites the reader to enter the discussion.

Since the first section in each chapter is Bible exploration the questions for group discussion are interspersed within the text to allow the flow of the argument to be examined. Study groups should pause at each question for discussion. In the second section of each chapter the questions are left to the end of the chapter. Study groups should read the section then look at these questions, choose those relevant to them, and also add their own topical questions on the same theme.

The book could therefore provide a four session Bible Study course if each member of the group arrived having read both sections of a chapter. An eight session course would be a more natural use of the book and, if serious consideration is to be given to all the questions involved, the course could last much longer. Individual readers will share the debate as they reflect on what they read.

## Chapter One

# The gospel story:
# The boy with epilepsy

Six days later Jesus took Peter, James, and John the brother of James, and led them up a high mountain where they were alone; and in their presence he was transfigured; his face shone like the sun, and his clothes became white as the light. And they saw Moses and Elijah appear, conversing with him. Then Peter spoke: 'Lord,' he said, 'how good it is that we are here! If you wish it, I will make three shelters here, one for you, one for Moses, and one for Elijah.' While he was still speaking, a bright cloud suddenly overshadowed them, and a voice called from the cloud: 'This is my Son, my Beloved, on whom my favour rests; listen to him.' At the sound of the voice the disciples fell on their faces in terror. Jesus then came up to them, touched them, and said, 'Stand up; do not be afraid.' And when they raised their eyes they saw no one, but only Jesus.

On their way down the mountain, Jesus enjoined them not to tell anyone of the vision until the Son of Man had been raised from the dead. The disciples put a question to him: 'Why then do our teachers say that Elijah must come first?' He replied, 'Yes, Elijah will come and set everything right. But I tell you that Elijah has already come, and they failed to recognise him, and worked their will upon him; and in the same way the Son of Man is to suffer at their hands.' Then the disciples understood that he meant John the Baptist.

**When they returned to the crowd, a man came up to Jesus, fell on his knees before him, and said, 'Have pity, sir, on my son: he is an epileptic and has bad fits, and he keeps falling about, often into the fire, often into the water. I brought him to your disciples, but they could not cure him.' Jesus answered, 'What an unbelieving and perverse generation! How long shall I be with you? How long must I endure you? Bring him here to me.' Jesus then spoke sternly to the boy; the devil left him, and from that moment he was cured.**

**Afterwards the disciples came to Jesus and asked him privately, 'Why could we not cast it out?' He answered, 'Your faith is too small. I tell you this: if you have faith no bigger even than a mustard seed, you will say to this mountain, "Move from here to there!", and it will move; nothing will prove impossible for you.'** *Matthew 17.1-20*

This familiar passage offers important evidence about the character of Jesus and his role in history. It outlines problems the disciples faced as they responded to the invitation to share Jesus' ministry. It interprets Jesus in the light of Jewish history and belief and also proclaims his unique relationship to God. Yet it is a human Jesus who speaks from the incident. He expresses frustration and almost disillusionment with the spiritual progress of his disciples. Jesus the teacher also emerges. He interprets the disciples' experience of John the Baptist, and explains the nature of faith.

The Transfiguration comes first, though a glance back to the immediately preceding verses of Matthew's gospel shows a clear and, in terms of time, an unusually precise link with the identification of Jesus as 'the Messiah, the Son of the living God'. Consequently there is recognition that both Jesus and his disciples will become suffering victims in a world that does not understand the nature of true Messiahship.

Matthew is the gospel writer who has Jewish readers mostly in mind. He clearly wants to promote a view of Jesus which sees him as culmination of the work of Moses and

Elijah. That is an understanding of the life and ministry of Jesus which will most commend him to Judaism. Moses, representing the Law, and Elijah, representative of all the prophets, talk with Jesus. Jesus shines within the moment. The other two disappear and Jesus is left with a confirming word from heaven that he has a special relationship - sonship, no less - with God; a relationship which neither Moses nor Elijah could claim. Something new has happened which does not deny either Law or Prophecy and which is clearly greater than both. All this would suit Matthew's purpose well as a gospel-writer who believes, and wants others to believe, that Jesus, though new and different, did not deny their history, culture, or essential beliefs but rather, transfigured and transformed them. We are clearly handling a seminal and evangelical passage.

Another important element in the incident lies in the fact that only Peter, James and John were present with Jesus. As patterns of authority developed in the early Church it was important to find evidence in the remembered life of Jesus which would authenticate the leadership and responsibilities of those who were guiding the emerging church. Peter and John appear often in the Book of Acts, James is given authority in the Church in Jerusalem. Matthew is suggesting that their leadership is natural and right because it had its roots in the lifetime of Jesus. They were the disciples who were closest to Jesus and shared his inner thoughts. If there was any power struggle in the early Church an earlier intimacy with Jesus would be a critical factor in its resolution. Even today, one sometimes hears Roman Catholics talk of Peter, James and John almost as though they were an embryonic Curia.

Educationalists can turn to this story with profit. They might see the three privileged disciples less in terms of status or office but find the language of 'readiness' more useful and ask why the three were ready for this experience and the

11

others were apparently not ready. They would need to look at the previous experience of the three, the dynamics of leadership within a group of twelve people, and many other factors. Mystics, on the other hand might read the passage and reflect on the nature of religious experience and how far the symbolism of light interprets Christian growth and experience.

What is the main meaning of this passage for you?

Then, of course, there is the familiar interpretation of the passage in which we see Jesus and the three coming from the mountain-top experience into the valley, there to meet the difficulties of normal earthly problems represented by the epileptic boy. Thus, many a preacher has told his congregation that we must leave the mountain-top experience of Sunday worship and engage in the ordinary life of the world each Monday. That sermon makes some assumptions about the nature of our Sunday worship which may not always be true. If Sunday worship is cold and irrelevant, lacking both wit and wisdom, the liveliness of Monday morning in school or work may seem more God-centred than any hour spent in church. Thus God often points his people to more midweek and seemingly secular mountain-tops in work, personal relationships, Christian service, and inner quietness than many a Sunday seems able to offer.

Are we always right to draw so sharp a distinction between Sunday and the rest of the week imagining that God operates more decisively in the one rather than the other? Share both Sunday and midweek experiences in which you have been confident of the action of God in your life.

But the story of the epileptic boy is a fascinating window into the life of the early Church. Look at the very end of the passage. The disciples had tried to heal the boy and had not been able. Jesus was able. The disciples ask the obvious question: Why could we not heal the boy when you could? Jesus gives them an answer: Your faith is too small. It sounds like a straightforward answer to a straightforward question. But is it quite as straightforward as that?

This is synoptic material. That is it appears in more than one of the gospel narratives of Matthew, Mark and Luke. In fact it appears in all three. It is thought to be originally Markan material which Luke and then Matthew use in their turn. There is a little adaptation of the material as it emerges in the three gospels but it does not change a great deal. One interesting change is in the response of Jesus.

Why couldn't we heal the boy?, ask the disciples when they are alone with Jesus. Interestingly, they seek a private discussion. Hoped for success and actual failure is the theme. Most of us prefer a discussion about our failures to be private rather than public.

> Is there any evidence that Christians find it difficult to admit failure? If so, what do you think the reasons are?

Jesus answers the disciples' question but curiously, Matthew, Mark, and Luke do not agree about what Jesus said. Compare the accounts written by the three writers.

**Afterwards the disciples came to Jesus and asked him privately, 'Why could we not cast it out?' He answered, 'Your faith is too small.'** *Matthew 17.19*

**Then Jesus went indoors, and his disciples asked him privately, 'Why could we not cast it out?' He said, 'There is no means of casting out this sort but prayer'** *Mark 9.28-29*

At this point in Mark's gospel the margin in some versions of the Bible, including the New English Bible, notes that some manuscripts say prayer *and* fasting. The same comment is made in the margin of some versions in Matthew's gospel.

There appear to be different testimonies about the response Jesus made and some indecision both across and within the gospel narratives.

So, comparing the narratives of Matthew and Mark we have Jesus offering three answers to the question. The disciples were unsuccessful because

1. they lacked faith
2. their prayers were inadequate, and
3. they should fast more.

How does Luke's narrative compare? He includes the story of the Transfiguration with much the same detail as the other two gospel writers. He also tells of the boy with epilepsy. As a medical man Luke records the symptoms of the boy's illness which Mark has noted but Matthew has abbreviated, recording that it makes him cry out suddenly, throws him into convulsions, and causes foaming at the mouth. But he does not record either the question of the disciples or the answer of Jesus. Instead he notes how the event elicits awe at the majesty of God. Is it the discretion - or perhaps the greater objectivity - of the doctor that makes him keep silent about the method of cure?

So we are left with three answers intermittently spread over manuscripts used by two Gospel writers. Why did the disciples fail? What is needed for success in these matters? Is it greater faith, more prayer, or fasting?

> To which of the three answers do you intuitively respond as being the reason for the disciples' failure?

If we are to take the Bible seriously these variations raise an important question which we can't avoid. How do you get three different answers? What did Jesus really say?

Are these three different occasions with three different epileptic boys about which Jesus said three different things? That seems unlikely. The narratives are so similar and follow on in each case so closely from the Transfiguration story that we must be reading about the same event.

Is it a case of bad memory or inadequate records with two of the writers of the various manuscripts illremembering the answer Jesus gave, and only one of them remembering accurately? In which case which is the right answer - the answer Jesus actually gave - and which two are wrong?

There is a third possibility which being simpler is also more likely: that we are overhearing a conversation.

Through these three diverse accounts are we listening in on a debate in the early Church? In the twentieth century Church we are often involved in discussion or argument from formal Assemblies, Synods and Church-meetings to informal discussion over coffee or after church services. Do we imagine that there was any less conversation and debate, or less disagreement in the early Church than in the Church of the twentieth century?

> Were the first Christians as fallible and perplexed as we are today? Would their proximity to the life of Jesus lessen their uncertainty?

The assumption behind this study book is that in these three different responses to the disciples' failure with the epileptic boy we have stumbled upon an item on the agenda of the early Church that exercised their minds in discussion and debate, and about which there were different opinions.

The agenda item was - why aren't we as successful as Jesus was? The question demanded an answer but there was disagreement among the first Christians about the right answer to give. At least three possible answers emerged.

It would be an important discussion. Exorcism and healings were, at least in the very early days a part of the assumptions of the early Church. Jesus had promised they would do greater things and presumably they sometimes found they could, and for reasons which our twentieth century knowledge of medicine and psychology might often be able to explain if we knew all the circumstances. But sometimes, more often than they liked, and contrary to their expectations, their attempts at healing failed. Being thoughtful people they had to ask why.

The 'why can't we heal people like Jesus did?' may be more their question than it is ours today, expectations being different. An appeal to the efficacy of medicine and drugs would be our first response rather than questions about prayer, fasting or faith. But it was a question they had to ask and since there was no obvious answer it led to debate - perhaps even argument - about it in the churches. Different traditions developed to explain their apparent failure. The different traditions became reflected in different manuscripts as they were written. Matthew captures and emphasises one tradition, Mark another. Perhaps Luke's 'no answer because there is no question' was yet another tradition.

We ought to pause for a moment because we are making some assumptions about the Bible which should be considered before we go further.

We tend to think of the Acts of the Apostles and the Letters of Paul as the documents which tell us about the early Church and the four gospels as documents which tell us about the life of Jesus. No one doubts that is the right emphasis. But we do disservice to the gospels until we recognise that they are documents not only *written* by the early Church but also *reflecting the priorities, insights, prejudices, hopes and internal debate of the early Church.*

Discuss your response to the last paragraph.

Many people using this study book will already realise that inevitably the Gospel writers saw the life of Jesus 'through their own spectacles' so that their personal experience, hopes, and fears influenced the way they told the story. The tragedy is that such an obvious understanding of the Bible is news to many in our congregations who hear the gospels read Sunday by Sunday almost with the assumption that they were written only from a 0-32 AD perspective by a reporter who followed Jesus everywhere he went, and who with precise accuracy wrote down everything Jesus said. There is a failure to recognise that the gospel narratives were powerfully influenced by a process of human reflection, church debate, and the personal experience of the writers throughout a period very much later than the life of Jesus. Naturally, his life was the most powerful influence on the early Church but it must not be forgotten that the gospel writers' experience of life in the early Church also greatly influenced the way they wrote about Jesus. The gospel narratives are not verbatim accounts of what Jesus said and did. They show the life of Jesus as seen through the eyes of the early Church.

One implication of this is that in the incident we are studying, as elsewhere in the gospels, we can no longer be absolutely sure what Jesus said in answer to a particular question though in the three possible answers we have a fascinating glimpse into an early Church debate. It turns the emphasis of the gospels away from being what-Jesus-said documents to being early-Church documents, or more accurately, early-Church-about-Jesus documents. The integrity of the gospel writers means that they would want us to hear him accurately. But we can never be as totally sure that they have been successful in their efforts as we would be if the gospels had been written by someone on the spot whose sole concern was to follow Jesus around from day to day and create an accurate account of all he said and did.

Taking this seriously, Bible study becomes less of a search for a finally authoritative answer to our human questions, but much more a willingness to enter into a debate, in which the early Church engaged, for which the early Christians offer us crucially important resources, and in which other generations later entered. We must in turn engage it. In all of this, as has often been said, we may not now hear the words of Jesus but we can hear his authentic voice.

> 'Bible study is the willingness to enter into a debate.' Discuss this statement. Is there an authoritative word within the debate we enter?

The connecting link across these studies is the recognition that the early Christians arrived at their faith and reached an understanding of the ministry of Jesus 'after much discussion'. That such discussion took place is clear. In the Acts of the Apostles and the Letters of Paul the debate between individual members of the Church, and groups of members on several issues is conspicuous and well documented.

For example, there was debate about the care of widows. It took place between two different language groups in the Church:

**During this period, when disciples were growing in number, there was disagreement between those of them who spoke Greek and those who spoke the language of the Jews. The former party complained that their widows were being overlooked in the daily distribution.** *See Acts 6.1*

To resolve the disagreement they appointed a group of people whose major task was to act in a serving role, leaving the apostles free to preach. It is a division of labour which some churches still maintain in the diaconate.

Similarly, there was an extensive debate in the early Church concerning whether new converts should be circumcised as Jews before being admitted into the Church. They had to decide whether Judaism was the only door into Christianity for everyone, as it had been for the first disciples who were all Jews before they were Christians.

**The apostles and elders held a meeting to look into this**

**matter.** *Acts 15.6.*

Peter was a principal speaker and argued that as God had given the Holy Spirit to Gentiles as well as to Jews they ought to be admitted.

**'We believe it is by the grace of the Lord Jesus that we are saved, and so are they.'** *Acts 15.11*

James appears to have chaired the meeting and sums up at the end.

**'My judgement therefore is that we should impose no irksome restrictions on those of the Gentiles who are turning to God'** *Acts 15.19*

The debate was sometimes personal and fierce. Paul recollects a serious disagreement with Peter which, unless he reneged on his earlier position, presumably took place before Peter himself welcomed Gentiles into the Church.

**But when Cephas (Peter) came to Antioch, I opposed him to the face, because he was clearly in the wrong. For until certain persons came from James he was taking his meals with gentile Christians; but when they came he drew back and began to hold aloof, because he was afraid of the advocates of circumcision.** *Galatians 2.11-12*

> Does it surprise you that the early Christians disagreed with each other and argued fiercely? How would they resolve their differences?

There are many other examples. The Corinthian correspondence shows widespread disagreement and argument between Paul and the church in Corinth. The Letter to the Colossians reflects an argument about the nature and centrality of Christ. The early Christians were seeking to hammer out their beliefs. It is unbelievable to imagine that in so doing they did not share in lengthy discussions often involving serious disagreement. Debate shouts from the pages of the Letters. An assumption behind these studies is that it is possible to detect the same arguments reflected in the stories and narrative of the gospels.

The incident of the epileptic boy in the gospels reveals one subject which created discussion in the early Church. The narrow debate about healing epilepsy now feels academic to us. How to cure epilepsy and why we are less successful in that and other medical fields raises more questions for us about National Health Service funding and the need for medical research than spiritual healing.

But the question of Christian success and Christian failure which lies behind the text is still with us. The debate which we can discern in the early Church continues in our time. That is the subject of the next section of this chapter.

# The wider debate:
# Christian success and failure

In the previous chapter the story of the epileptic boy revealed a debate in the early Church about their failure to effect healing. Three strands of the debate were identified in the gospels written by Matthew and Mark. We fail, they said

- because we lack faith
- because we do not pray as we ought
- because we do not fast as we should.

The debate now becomes our own. Why aren't we more successful than we are - in mission, in changing the world, in growing up to Christian maturity, in our perception of the purposes of God, in the whole life of the Church? Think of our resources: the riches of Christ, the 'more than we can ask or think' of God's gifts.

Manifestly, we fail. We can sympathise with the man who, having listened to an Easter Day sermon telling the glory of that resurrection in which we all share and a Pentecost sermon on the free availability of the resources of the Spirit, looked around the church and asked why it wasn't working! Was the preacher in danger of prosecution under the Trades Description Act?

Why do we fail? We will examine each of the ideas the early Church arrived at and then consider the ways in which some contemporary Christians are involving themselves in the same debate.

First, we are not successful, said one group, because we don't pray aright. Charles Elliott contributes to that debate in his book, *'Praying the Kingdom'* where he is concerned about the success and failure of the Church in its response to world poverty, and makes a plea for more prayer.

Not the prayer, he suggests, which becomes 'little more than a political shopping list, a platform, a manifesto.' He offers a burlesque example:

*May we have a more humane policy on unemployment; and that, Lord, means a proper balance of Keynesian and monetarist policies; more resources on training and labour mobility . . . Oh, and Lord, don't forget to do something about the exchange rate.*

Then, Charles Elliott, linking prayer with an identification with people in their need, goes to the root of the question, asking:

*I am well aware that I am very English, middle-class, slightly intellectual, shy, a clergyman . . . How can I genuinely identify with striking miners in South Wales and starving peasants in Mali. To welcome them into my home would be more embarrassing for them than for me. To stand alongside them would amuse them for its incongruity. Like Dr. Johnson's dog, they would marvel not that I did it well or naturally, but that I did it at all. Try as I might, I cannot be other than I am. For better or worse, this is what God made me and I have trouble enough coming to terms with that, without trying to be something quite other.*

*And yet, . . . And yet, unless I am moving towards that degree of empathy, of friendliness, of readiness to share that would culminate in a real welcome, actual standing alongside, there is little prospect of my being able to open myself to the poor at a deeper, more inward level. . . . the call to pray for the Kingdom is a call to know, to be acquainted with, the poor and marginalised in our own community.*

When such identification with others becomes our style of praying, prompted by a debate the first Christians began when they failed to help a young boy, and enriched by the experience of a contemporary Christian who struggles to stand alongside the poor, perhaps we are beginning to understand the nature of success - and failure.

Secondly, a group in the early Church suggested: We are not successful because we don't fast enough.

That may mean a few more austerity lunches during Christian Aid Week, and living more simply that others may simply live. That, but more than that.

> *For is not this*
> *the fast that I have chosen*
> *(the prophet spoke)*
> *to shatter every yoke,*
> *of wickedness*
> *the grievous bands to loosen,*
> *oppression put to flight*
> *to fight till every wrong's set right.*
> > *Then shall your light*
> > *break forth as doth the morning . . .*

and so hymn writer Percy Dearmer contributes to the debate, calling on the testimony of one of the authors of the Book of Isaiah *(Isaiah 58.5-12)* and points us to a new kind of fasting which is concerned less with minimising food and more with maximising justice. It asks not only that we eat less but that we share. Fasting in Isaiah's day was marked by lying on a bed of sackcloth and ashes and hoping that such flamboyant attitudes would attract the attention of God. Isaiah redefined fasting in social and political terms rather than purely personal terms:

> **Is not this what I require of you as a fast:**
> **to loose the fetters of injustice,**
> **to untie the knots of the yoke,**
> **to snap every yoke**
> **and set free those who have been crushed?**
> **Is it not sharing your food with the hungry**
> **taking the homeless poor into your house,**
> **clothing the naked when you meet them**
> **and never evading a duty to your kinsfolk?**
>
> *Isaiah 58.6-7*

What does 'success' mean if we take that seriously? Such a fast would lead to a very different kind of success than that which we often seek. It would mean less food, less clothing, and less opportunity - so that others may have more. It is not the kind of success with which commerce and industry tempt their new managerial recruits. It represents neither the goals that are held out before sixth formers on Prize Day nor the ambitions most parents present to their children. But our familiar ideas about success may nurture the seeds of failure judged by the Gospel whilst the willingness to fail in the world's estimation may count as Gospel success.

Thirdly, Matthew had listened to another group in the early Church and recalls their plea that success was at their fingertips - if only they had faith enough.

Fr Harry Williams enters the debate at that point in his book *'True Wilderness'*

*Faith consists in the acceptance of doubt, not, as we generally think, in its repression*

Or coming at it in another way: What is the opposite of faith? We instinctively choose 'doubt' as the opposite of 'faith', but faith is a word that lends itself to several opposites: despair, lack of confidence, unbelief, lack of trust, sight etc. All these are contenders alongside 'doubt' as faith's opposite.

Another opposite of faith is certainty. Faith assumes openness and pilgrimage. Faith is prepared to walk without sight but with hope. Faith is 'commitment within un-certainty'. The author of the Letter to the Hebrews identifies faith as the response that allowed Abraham to set out for the land which God had promised for him and leave home 'without knowing where he was to go' *(Hebrews 11.8)*. Faith of this kind took Jesus through his life and as far as Calvary, not knowing what the eventual outcome was to be.

It is certainty that kills faith. Tightly closed creeds which think they have caught the faith in formulae of words are faith-destroying. It is the assumption of success in the way the world counts success that denies faith. Faith asks a different set of questions. It keeps doors open that certainty would close. The wilderness of Gethsemane-uncertainty is more the place of that success which faith brings, than is the tarmaced road of certainty offered by some popular evangelists.

Jesus, of course, is a major contributor to the debate about Christian success and failure. Looked at from our normal point of view the gospels represent him throughout as a failure. His parents lived in one of the less respected areas of Israel. The gospel writers represent his origins and life-style in a story of his birth in humble circumstances, and in a manger-bed. His education was limited. Largely ignored during his lifetime his occasional popularity was always insecure. He died an ignominious death between two thieves. Marginalised in his lifetime he was crucified outside the city walls and buried in a borrowed grave. If that is the story of success then most of us would welcome failure.

In any Christian discussion about the nature of success this man must become a partner in the debate. Once invited he will probably arrive on a donkey and there will be the shadow of a cross in his eyes. Let him speak about the nature of Christian success and failure.

**Questions for group discussion**

1  Who is more successful - the young person whose salary rises by leaps and bounds or the one who deliberately chooses a poorly paid job in a service-agency? What are the criteria for success in employment? Are the highly paid more successful in a Christian sense if they are generous to charities?

2  Twenty to thirty people meet each week in a dwindling congregation in a church which was once well-attended and successful. Now it is surrounded by light industries, waste ground, and only a few houses. They debate their future. Some argue that the witness must continue in the place where history has placed them, regardless of the odds; others that realism means they must disperse to other congregations; others say their presence in a difficult area is prophetic and their time will come again. What advice would you give the meeting?

3  'The call to pray for the Kingdom is a call to know, to be acquainted with, the poor and marginalised in our own community' Charles Elliott. Is that true? What is the place and purpose of more traditional acts of prayer? How would you define 'successful praying'?

4  In what way was Jesus Christ a success?

5  Work through the various opposites of faith suggested in this chapter listing reasons why they should or should not be thought of as faith's opposites. Which seems to you to be the most appropriate as an opposite?

6  Discuss and then list the criteria of success for a local church. Is your church a successful church by these standards?

7  Using Isaiah's understanding of fasting write a paragraph for the church magazine inviting people to a fast.

## Chapter Two

# The gospel story:
# The coin in the fish's mouth

On their arrival at Capernaum the collectors of the temple-tax came up to Peter and asked, 'Does your master not pay temple-tax?' 'He does', said Peter. When he went indoors Jesus forestalled him by asking, 'What do you think about this, Simon? From whom do earthly monarchs collect tax or toll? From their own people, or from aliens?' 'From aliens', said Peter. 'Why then,' said Jesus, 'their own people are exempt! But as we do not want to cause offence, go and cast a line in the lake; take the first fish that comes to the hook, open its mouth, and you will find a silver coin; take that and pay it in; it will meet the tax for us both.

*Matthew 17.24-27*

The second passage from the Bible that we study virtually follows on from the one we considered in the previous two chapters.

Is that a coincidence or are they connected by the question, how do Christians live in the reality of day-to-day experience? That question must include, as we saw from the previous chapter, another question namely, how do we, who have the resources of Christ at our disposal, live with the reality of failure? The related question for this next study becomes, how do we live with the reality of earthly powers with whose philosophy we may or may not agree?

To reach that question we must go step by step. What

kind of biblical material are we studying in this section?

It could be a simple account of one incident in the life of Jesus. The suggestion that Peter will find a coin in a fish's mouth might be interpreted as a miracle or as an explanation telling how, from time to time, whether for daily food or for special purposes such as taxes the disciples used those skills and abilities - fishing, carpentry etc - which had once been their full-time means of self-support. If so, then like Paul with his tent-making, Peter here drops back on his old fishing trade to raise a spot of ready cash to pay the tax.

Alternatively, the story might have begun its life as one more of the many parables Jesus told and which, in the course of early Church preaching and remembrance was turned into a story about Jesus as though it had actually happened. Historical incident or parable, the gospel-writers' use of it opens a further window onto the early Church and allows us to share in another of the first century debates which is still relevant for us in the twentieth century.

What kind of a story do you think this is?
- an accurate historic record of an actual incident?
- an explanation of how the disciples earned money to support Jesus and themselves?
- a parable which Jesus once told which, through much telling, became a story about Jesus?

The background is this. It was an almost universal custom among Jews not only in Palestine but all over the Roman Empire to pay an annual tax of a half shekel for the upkeep of the temple. The amount was equivalent to about two days wages for a labourer.

It was a poll tax. It did not relate to income. Rich and poor paid the same, which means of course, that the poor paid relatively more. Few governments take full account of the fact that all such taxes make the rich relatively richer and the poor relatively poorer.

The tax for the temple upkeep was a voluntary tax although a good deal of moral and religious pressure was used to encourage people to pay it. In fact there was some debate about it. The tax derived from a passage in Exodus. **The Lord spoke to Moses and said: When you number the Israelites for the purposes of registration, each man shall give a ransom for his life to the Lord, to avert plague among them during the registration. As each man crosses over to those already counted he shall give half a shekel by the sacred standard (twenty gerahs to the shekel) as a contribution to the Lord . . . The rich man shall give no more than the half-shekel, and the poor man shall give no less, when you give the contribution to the Lord to make expiation for your lives. The money received from the Israelites for expiation you shall apply to the service of the Tent of the Presence.** *Exodus 30.11-16*

The Pharisees and Sadducees disagreed about the tax as over much else. The Sadducees noted that in Exodus it was a one-off payment for a particular registration of the people rather than a recurring payment. They argued that the now expected annual payment of tax towards the temple upkeep was a later tradition rather than a permanent Mosaic rule, and thus with their usual pedantry enjoyed the debate about whether it should be paid or not.

The Pharisees, on the other hand, took the line that even if this was not originally a regular payment it had now become permanent by established tradition and so everyone should pay it as though it was a matter of law.

It is the kind of argument we still hear amongst Christians. For us it might emerge as a debate between a fundamentalist approach which looks to the original documents to define truth for all time, as against those who believe there is an ongoing revelation of the mind of God to which ancient perceptions of the truth must adjust.

A major division in the Church over the centuries has centred on the relative authority of the Bible and tradition. Some have argued that the Bible is definitive for all time, others that the way the Church has developed over the centuries carries its own authority.

> Are the practices and beliefs of the early Church authoritative for us? Do we have to copy them as closely as possible? If so, why?
>
> Does God speak through the way practice and belief has developed? How do we test whether tradition is good or bad? What do we do when what we read in the Bible appears to be different from what we are now doing and believing?

Pastor John Robinson spoke to the pilgrims on the 'Mayflower' as they set sail for America in 1620:

*For my part I cannot sufficiently bewail the condition of the Reformed Churches, who are come to a period in religion and will go no farther than the instruments of their reformation. The Lutheran can't be drawn to go beyond what Luther says; and the Calvinists, you see, stick fast where they were left by that great man of God, who yet saw not all things. I beseech you, remember, 'tis an Article of your Church Covenant, that you be ready to receive whatever truth shall be made known to you . . . He charged us before God and his blessed angels, to follow him no farther than he followed Christ. And if God should reveal anything to us by another instrument of his, to be as ready to receive it, as ever we were to receive any truth by his ministry, for he was very confident the Lord had more truth and light yet to break forth out of his holy Word.*

The Sadducees would not have approved of such a statement; the Pharisees would have applauded it. The question to Jesus, therefore, is not so much 'Are you a law abiding person who pays his taxes?' as 'What is your theological judgment on this matter? Is this a permanent tax or a one-off payment which people need repeat now only if they wish to do so?' Jesus' answer would reveal whether he stood with the Sadducees or the Pharisees.

That makes it not unlike other questions he was asked, such as the one the Sadducees asked Jesus about resurrection *(Luke 20.27-38)* to try to get him to refute the notion of resurrection in which the Pharisees believed. They told the trick story of the women who would have ended up in heaven with seven potential husbands because each of seven brothers died one by one and the law required the next youngest brother to marry her. Which one would be the heavenly husband? In both cases Jesus did what he so often did, and refused to answer in the expected terms.

In the story before us Jesus forestalls Peter's question, and getting his own questions in first, broadens the issue from the simple matter of collecting the temple tax to a more general discussion about our relationship to authority. 'From whom do earthly monarchs collect taxes?' - and so on.

Had he not done so the story would hardly have been preserved by Matthew. It is the fact that it touches on an important matter the early Church had to face up to that constrained Matthew to include it in his gospel. Similarly, it is doubtful whether the gospel writers would have preserved the record of strife between Pharisees and Sadducees about resurrection except that resurrection became such a critically important theme in the early Church. Any reference to it became important, especially when associated with a comment by Jesus.

Remember the essential idea behind this study book. Knowing that we can readily see debate in the early Church in the Acts of the Apostles and the Letters of Paul, and recognising that the period of writing the gospels either overlaps or post-dates the letters, we are looking for evidence of early Church debate in the pages of the gospels. We recognise that the gospels are not simply 'life of Jesus' documents, but also 'life of the early Church' documents reflecting the hopes, fears, prejudices and wrestling of a young Church in debate for the truth.

Can we hear an early Church discussion behind this story of the coin in the fish's mouth? I believe we can. This story too can become a window through which we read an item on the early Church's agenda.

What is the subject of the debate that lies behind this narrative?

It could be about whether the early Christians should continue to pay the temple tax.

That would be a pressing question for Christians out of the Jewish tradition. They had been brought up to pay it, but as their initial dual 'daily attendance at the temple and breaking bread in private houses' *(Acts 2.46-47)* yielded to a Christian community in which the Jewish temple was less and less important, the question necessarily arose about their financial support of the temple. When they were worshipping regularly in the temple as Jews it was fair to pay for its upkeep. But the temple became less and less important as the focus of their worship. Furthermore they developed other financial responsibilities such as the care of widows in their own Christian community, the help they gave to travelling evangelists like Paul and the assistance for the poor in Jerusalem which Paul initiated. With limited resources they had to decide on their priorities.

The question belongs to other ages as well. In the nineteenth century Norfolk farmers who were Dissenters and had left the Church of England still had to pay a tithe for the upkeep of the parish church. Why should they, they argued, when their loyalty and consequent financial support had been transferred to the village Congregational, Baptist or Methodist chapel?

Similarly, at the end of the last century, once they had the Citadel to upkeep why should Salvationists make any contribution to the Methodist or other church they had attended before?

Even if in more polite terms, the same questions are asked now in some Local Ecumenical Projects where the old denominational allegiances are less important but decisions still have to be made about the financial support of the several denominational parents, denominational missionary societies, women's, and youth organisations.

> Discuss any occasion when members of the group have resented being asked to support a cause or organisation that had become irrelevant to their lives. What principles guided their eventual decision?

Back to the first century. If important for first century *Jewish* Christians, for first century *Gentile* Christians the question was even more acute. They had taken on board a lot of Jewish luggage already - Jewish language, Jewish thought-forms, Jewish patterns of worship, a set of Jewish sacred books which, until much later and the advent of the New Testament, were the dominant literature of the early Church, and a Jewish perspective of history. Must they also take on the Jewish temple tax? It must have seemed an unfair, almost ridiculous suggestion.

The contemporary ecumenical situation is relevant again. The first century Gentiles stand alongside those new Christian converts today who, being brought up in an ecumenical community and having had no previous denominational allegiance, find the denominational thought forms and assumptions irksome. They are being asked to pay an emotional tax for a temple they have never experienced.

In ecumenical study groups relate the last paragraph to your own experience.

Perhaps, therefore, in the coin in the fish's mouth story we are hearing a debate around the agenda item: Should we pay the temple tax when we no longer feel any commitment to the temple?

It may be, however, that we are hearing an even more important debate for in fact, by the time Matthew had written his gospel the temple had been destroyed and the temple tax, as such, was no longer a living issue. Further, this story only appears in Matthew's gospel.

If we accept the argument that Mark wrote his gospel *before* AD 70, and thus before the destruction of the temple, and that Matthew wrote his gospel *after* AD 70 and thus after the destruction of the temple this might provide a reason why the story appeals to Matthew but fails to attract Mark. Had the destruction of the temple removed the superficial discussion about half-shekels and put a new and sharper edge on a wider issue which obliged Matthew to comment on a story which Mark could afford to ignore? What is that wider issue?

What happened to the temple tax when there was no temple? Governments do not readily abandon taxes. In this case the temple tax which was a Jewish tax was conveniently added to other taxes imposed by Rome, and thus became a Roman tax. And, as you might imagine, Rome was not interested in the niceties of whether the Book of Exodus was outlining a permanent or ad hoc tax. Rome simply said: pay.

Thus the debate we are now overhearing in this story is not simply about whether we should contribute to the building fund of that other religious group down the road we used to belong to. The story and the tax point to a more acute question about the Church's relationship to the State since the tax is now imposed by a ruling, alien power.

The item for debate in the early Church has widened as this chapter has proceeded. Note the stages:

1 Does Jesus support the Sadducee or the Pharisee position on temple tax?

2 Should the first Jewish Christians continue to support the upkeep of the temple when their loyalty to temple worship was decreasing and moving toward the house church described in the Acts of the Apostles?

3 Should Gentile Christians who had never supported the temple be obliged to do so now that they had become Christians?

4 Now that the tax has become a Roman rather than Jewish tax should Christians whose allegiance is to the Kingdom of God not the Roman Empire pay the tax of an alien power whose policies were so often alien to Christian perceptions?

In the debate discerned in the story of the epileptic boy it was possible to see the three parties in the argument represented in three different gospels, almost as though Matthew, Mark and Luke were individual speakers leading discussion in a church meeting.

The debate this time however, is internal to the narrative before us and caught up in one piece of evidence - the account Matthew gives us. How many different voices can we hear in this account?

It is doubtful whether Matthew is enabling us to hear every expression of early Church opinion on the subject. Some radical must have said, 'Roman tax? Not on your life! You cannot serve God and Mammon.'

Wouldn't someone else have advised caution? 'Leave it be. Let's get on with the job of winning souls and leave things like taxes and politics to those who know more about them.'

Even so, it is possible to hear at least three strands of the argument in Matthew's narrative. *Verse 25* offers the first.

**'Does your Master not pay temple-tax?'**

**'He does', said Peter.**

That is an unequivocal answer of the kind that might have come from a member of the early Church arguing that it was better to pay up, keep a low profile, and get on with the more important spiritual task.

*Verse 26* enters a second strand in the debate. The varying tax responsibilities of citizens and aliens is noted.

**'From whom do earthly monarchs collect tax or toll? From their own people, or from aliens?'**

**'From aliens', said Peter.**

**'Why then', said Jesus, 'their own people are exempt!'**

Jesus is still laying claim to the temple. Owners do not pay toll on their own property. It is one side of the ambivalence of the young Church about its link with the old forms of worship. Does this suggest that there was one group in the early Church which argued that since the Jewish authorities had rejected God's Messiah, Judaism now had no claim on the temple itself and that Christians, by their obedience to the Messiah, were the rightful inheritors of the temple building where worship, reformed by the teaching and life of Jesus could be offered in spirit and in truth? Dissidents who secede like to take their buildings with them.

But the consensus view seems to emerge in *verse 27*: 'Pay up so that we do not cause offence'. The words are on the lips of Jesus, and the gospel writer's integrity means that if he put them there it is the judgment he believed Jesus either did, or would have, made.

It is unlikely that Matthew is suggesting that Jesus' comment would have been: 'Look, let's not cause any trouble. We might get hurt if we do. We don't agree with it, but let's pay up and look cheerful'. Jesus was willing to 'give offence' at other times and laissez-faire politicians, moralists, and religious leaders usually die comfortably in their beds, not on crosses.

Presumably the message is much more: In the great struggle for the establishment of the Kingdom of God we should choose our battlefields with care. Fight there will be, but choose the issue worth fighting for. A tax worth a couple of days wages isn't the one to choose.

Not that the amount was critical. Principle is more important. But in the believer's struggle against an alien power the choice of arena is part of Christian political discipline. And the debate inherent in this text is a political issue about the Church's relationships to the State to which, at this stage in its life, the early Church gave a tactical answer.

The original temple tax debate thus becomes: 'How do Christians relate to secular authorities?' No one ought to be surprised to hear an echo of that debate in the gospels. It is clearly there in the Acts of the Apostles and the letters Paul wrote - and the same ambivalence is there, too.

In one passage Paul pushes it to an extreme which could be dangerously compromising in that he makes the State a direct agent of God.

**Every person must submit to the supreme authorities. There is no authority but by act of God, and the existing authorities are instituted by him; consequently anyone who rebels against authority is resisting a divine institution, and those who so resist have themselves to thank for the punishment they will receive. For government, a terror to crime, has no terrors for good behaviour.** *Romans 13.1-3*

That may have been sound advice if Paul was writing in a period of a benevolent government committed to justice and human rights. Would he say the same when the government of the day was oppressive of human freedom? The world has known too many governing authorities that have been terrors to good behaviour but offered no terror to oppressors.

It was much later before Christians were emancipated from the doctrine of the divine right of kings, as witness the personal agonies of Cromwell and his dissenting contemporaries as they wrestled with the question of whether a king could be impeached of treason against the people. In our own century the Americans felt no such moral dilemma in dealing with President Nixon's involvement in the Watergate scandal perhaps because America was itself born out of rebellion against an authority which they saw to be oppressive and unjust.

But the other important side of the biblical debate is put by Peter. Faced by the supreme authorities he enters a different argument.

**So they brought them and stood them before the Council; and the High priest began his examination. 'We expressly ordered you', he said, 'to desist from teaching in that name; and what has happened? You have filled Jerusalem with your teaching, and you are trying to make us responsible for that man's death.' Peter replied for himself and the apostles: 'We must obey God rather than men'.**

*Acts 5.27-29*

Are all existing authorities instituted by God? Can appointed governments ever be disobeyed or plotted against? If so, under what circumstances?

Can the views of Paul and Peter on this matter be reconciled or is the Bible itself a book that invites its readers to struggle with ambivalence, and asks questions as well as giving some answers?

This book is based on a series of Bible studies first shared with the General Assembly of the United Reformed Church, a church which unites the three strands of Congregationalism, Presbyterianism and the Churches of Christ. Its roots therefore lie in British Protestant Dissent and the seventeenth century struggle of a group of Christians to be free of the constraints the State and the Established Church was making on them in their worship and mission. If the forbears of those who shared the Assembly Bible Study entered the debate about a Christian's relationship to the State it would be to stand with Peter rather than Paul and argue that being Christian means that we always face secular authority with questions on our lips. Their churchmanship was born out of rebellion against the 'existing authorities'. Many of their successors would still regard an Established Church, interlocking with the State at many critical points as both curious and potentially dangerous to Christian integrity.

Put the debate this way. In our acts of worship we sing 'We praise, we worship Thee, O God'. We declare, 'Jesus is Lord'. We sit at a table eating bread and drinking wine, an event which is at one and the same time a commemoration of a man who died unjustly at the hands of legal but bad authorities, and also an event commemorating the birth of the Israelite nation struggling to be free of tyrannous Egyptian authority. Having done these things we forever after approach any other authority with some caution. The claim of another kingdom, a greater authority is too close to us.

> What are the political implications of an act of Christian worship which proclaims God as the central and ultimate authority in our lives?

The relationship of the Church to State authority is a matter which must remain high on the ecumenical agenda. In ecumenical discussions we recognise the need to reconcile our differences in such matters as the ordination of women, different liturgical habits, and episcopacy. We have also to face up to the relationship between Church and State and whether the new ecumenical church would be Established or Free. A united church that fudged that question would be severed again within a generation.

These are questions that take us into our own time and lead us to the next chapter.

*Chapter Two continued*

# The wider debate:
# Christian responses to authority

The early Church began our debate about authority. In the story of the coin in the fish's mouth it moved from a relatively simple matter of whether the disciples should pay a half-shekel for the temple upkeep to the more difficult question of the relationship of the emerging Church to the State authorities. We heard Peter and Paul putting alternative views. Let our contemporaries share this debate the early Church began.

One voice can be represented by a memorial plaque in the Wilhelm Kaiser Gedächtnis Kirche in Berlin. It is a memorial to Germans who died in the Second World War. British visitors expect, as they look at it to see the familiar dates 1939-1945. In fact it reads 1932-1945, a reminder of the longer struggle of some German Christians with a duly appointed but evil authority. The Nazi period of the 1930's saw the German Protestant Church divided. The Nazi's sponsored the *Deutsche Christen* a church that tried to bring about a synthesis between Nazism and Christianity. They secured the support of more than half the German Church during the Second World War.

The Confessing Church took a different view and opposed Hitler and his Nazis. In 1933 Pastor Martin Niemöller founded the 'Pastor's Emergency League'. In the following year they set up alternative church authorities in areas where the official church was *Deutsche Christen* and produced the Barmen Declaration, a statement of faith which became their foundation document of Christian witness against 'Nazi Christianity'.

Consider their struggle in the early to middle 1930's. How did the Confessing church know when to resist, when to play it cool, and when to scream at the distress and falsehood in the nation? The German church was violently torn in its response to Hitler. The Peter argument: We must obey God not man, and the Paul argument: submit to the existing authorities were both heard, and the church divided on the issue.

And us? The British situation is in a much lower key but the debate on the Church's relationship with the State still goes on. The Bishop of Durham chose his sermon on Easter Day 1988 as the opportunity to criticise the British Government's change of policy on social benefits. He judged that the Government's policies, linked with a refusal to take note of criticism brought them to a position of being 'almost wicked'. The Bishop of Peterborough, took a different view and was critical of his bishop-colleague. One Conservative M.P. called the Bishop of Durham 'a fool and an anti-Christ', and the Chairman of the Conservative Party appealed for Church and State to keep out of each other's affairs.' Those elements heard within the Church of England debate were also echoed in other churches.

Whether the Church should involve itself closely in politics has pervaded church discussions throughout the 1980's. It is the same question in a different context that the German Christians faced in the 1930's. It will arise again and again in future decades. It is a critical debate in a democracy. If the people have elected a government has a Christian the right to express widespread criticism of its actions? On the other hand, if the duly appointed government is perceived to be 'almost wicked' can Christians be silent?

The question will always arise in specific instances and there will rarely be one simple and clear answer to the prevailing problem. For example, has the Church any legitimate comment to make about widespread unemployment? To become involved takes us into areas of economic development and control, where theology may fear to tread. If, on these grounds we are silent, what do we say to the individual unemployed person whose family is suffering because there is no work?

Similarly, if, as many Christians do, we believe that the National Health Service is an expression of Christian care and justice, do we protest when a hospital ward is closed or wait till it's the hospital itself that shuts its doors? If there is a queue of elderly ladies waiting for hip-joint replacements is that a matter for Christian conscience and thus Christian rebuke of those who control the finances and could reduce the waiting lists?

Is the degree and manner of taxation purely a matter for governments to decide or has the Church the right or duty to reflect on the effect of taxation and make moral comments on government tax policy? Before both the 1987 and 1988 Budgets surveys revealed a consensus amongst the British public that showed a willingness to forego tax cuts in favour of additional funds for the National Health Service. The Government arguing that it was already well supporting the National Health Service, judged that the long-term effect of tax cuts would be a better incentive to the growth of national prosperity than further funding of the Health Service. How should the Church re-act to this? Does it discover 'a word from God' in the mind of the people or the policy of the Government?

'When' is often the critical word. Should the Confessing Church in Germany have re-acted before it did? Does the Church wait until the unemployment list is 1 million long or five million long? Choosing the time for battle with the appointed authorities is as difficult and critical as choosing the arena. The clinging suspicion in British Christianity is that, loving a kind of peace as we do, we wait too long before we respond. We are very patient and cautious even when our patience is contributing to the hurt of the poor. As with general criticism, the 'when' is made all the more difficult in a democracy which re-elects its government every five years. There is a logic in the argument which says that the government having been democratically elected, dissidents to its policy must wait for the next five-year opportunity to change the direction. There is also the argument that in such matters as taxation or the decline of medical care there comes a point of no return so that a later government would be unable to redress injustice.

The challenge rarely comes to the Church corporately. It usually falls on individuals. As John Foster makes clear, the issue often presented itself in personal terms in that period in Germany which is so useful an example of Church/State relationships because the issues were so stark.

*Already in 1940 the order had gone out. Incurables and the insane were no longer to be a burden on the Reich. Three high officials descended upon the Bethel institution (a huge hospital for epileptics and the mentally ill). 'Herr Pastor', they said, 'the Fuehrer has decided that all these people must be gassed.' Von Bodelschwingh looked at them calmly. 'You can put me in a concentration camp, if you want; that is your affair. But so long as I am free you do not touch one of my patients. I cannot change to fit the times or wishes of the Fuehrer. I stand under orders from our Lord Jesus Christ.'*

from *'What are the Churches Doing'*

In calmer circumstances but handling equally important issues Beryl Hibbs and Maisie Birmingham can share the debate. Quakers, they were employed at Friends House, and were brought before the court in 1985 for withholding £2745 from the inland revenue - that being the sum 33 headquarters staff should have contributed through tax to military preparations and armaments. They were arguing for a peace tax which would allow those opposed to military force to provide money, by tax, for peaceful purposes. They argued that the conscientious objection allowed in wartime should extend to peacetime so that, just as wartime objectors can divert their energy and time to activities that do not directly contribute to the war effort so, in peacetime, they should be allowed to divert their taxes from war-preparation to peace-building.

Various groups in Scotland faced a similar issue by the introduction of the Poll Tax (Community Charge). Groups as varied as the Scottish National Party, the Scottish Labour Party, and the Student Christian Movement in Scotland contemplated refusing to register as the law required. Such an action would be illegal but, in view of the injustice of a Poll Tax, does it become a moral imperative?

The coin in the fish's mouth has become both contemporary and political. The Bible is a political book as well as being a book concerned with private morality and personal, spiritual growth.

The debate is universal to the Church. In 1961 Martin Luther King set himself, and called others to follow him, in opposing the authority of the United States of America in its treatment of its black citizens. He chose his weapons with care. They were the weapons of non-violence. Of the democratically elected authorities he said:

*'They can put you in a dungeon and transform you to glory. If they try to kill you, develop a willingness to die . . . We will win with the power of our capacity to endure.'*

The laws and practices that kept blacks and whites rigidly segregated, and the blacks in a position of subservience, had been unchallenged in the southern states of the U.S.A. for generations. By non-violence Luther King gained a moral authority over the representatives of the legal and social system and sowed the seeds that eventually brought forth justice. Luther King offers a contribution both to the 'when' and the 'how' of dissidence. His method was one which had already been used to good effect by Gandhi against the British in both South Africa and India and which is still being used in South Africa by Bishop Desmond Tutu and Dr Allan Boesak amongst others.

The Christian Church in East Germany today can enter the debate with its contribution of 'critical solidarity' in relationship to the State. The Church needs to be in 'solidarity' with the State because common citizenship and proper patriotism demand it but it is also 'critical' because Christians have an allegiance which always overrides our allegiance to the existing authorities.

Finally, to come nearer home, the debate can be taken into the life of the Church itself. For the individual Christian the Church stands as an authority demanding its temple tax of obedience and loyalty. What do you do if you believe the policy of your own church, local or national, to be in error?

You could follow one strand of the argument in this Matthew narrative: We do not want to cause offence so we remain silent, and obedient. Even if it seemed necessary, which thank God it is not, no one would want to make every item in a church meeting or Synod a battlefield. Though with no Church assembly having infallibility the times must come when Peter's argument 'We must obey God rather than man' overrides Paul's acceptance of all authority - even Church authority - as God's authority.

If ever the crunch comes in the life of a church the Christian rebel against church authority, once he or she has taken seriously every comment of the corporate church, has only one thing to fall back on in the end - that most dangerous though highly treasured authority of an individual perception of the mind of Christ - whilst looking, if with great trepidation, for whatever resources for survival can be found in the nearest fish's mouth.

**For group discussion**

1 Role-play a small group in Germany at the outset of Nazi rule. Different members should take the following roles:
   a this is an alien philosophy which will destroy the life of the Church and ultimately deny God himself. Therefore it must be boldly opposed no matter what the consequences.
   b the Church has to live in the real world and accommodate itself to different ideologies so we must co-operate.
   c since the survival of the Church is crucial then without actually denying our conscience we will try to steer a middle way knowing that our time will come again.
   d we must organise an underground church.
   e however seemingly alien, this State authority represents the authority of God for us in our time and we must obey it.

2 Invite one of your group to introduce a policy of the government about which he or she has conscientious disagreement. Does the group agree? If not, how do you reach a common mind?

3 Discuss the peace tax issue trying to understand why the two Quakers supported it and the government refused to introduce it.

4 'Once democratically elected on a Manifesto a government must be allowed its policies. Any protest denies democracy.' Discuss.

5 Is the phrase 'critical solidarity', created to describe relationships between Church and State, helpful in describing relationships between individual members and the wider Church.

6 Read the final section of the chapter. What dangers arise from relying on a personal understanding of the mind of Christ?

7 Several recent British governments have been elected by less than 50 per cent of the voters. Does this justify those who actively oppose them? Is it less right to oppose a government with a clear majority?

## *The Celebrating Series*

### Festival Services for various occasions

Arising from discussions between leaders of various age-groups within the church, Donald Hilton has written this series of booklets offering Festival Services for special occasions throughout the Church year.

Titles in this series include:
*Celebrating Christmas Books 1&2*
*Celebrating Special Sundays*
*Celebrating Lent and Easter Bk 1*
*Celebrating Harvest.*

## *Talking Together Series*

### Study material for House Groups

Written to spark off discussion, reflection and action in House-groups, Donald Hilton's booklets offer a wealth of study material giving each of your sessions new ideas for faith-building and further learning.

Also in this series:
*Raw Materials of Faith*
*Risks of Faith*
*Results of Faith*

### SEND FOR COMPLETE LIST

## National Christian Education Council
Robert Denholm House, Nutfield, Redhill, Surrey RH1 4HW

## Chapter Three

# The gospel story:
# The Canaanite woman

In alternate years, and moving from major city to major city in West Germany, the German Protestant Church holds its Kirchentag. A small number of British visitors usually attend. In 1985 it was held in Düsseldorf. The Kirchentag is difficult to describe to anyone who hasn't been. It's a carnival and a musical festival but also a conference in which high-powered theologians from across the world deliver lectures and lead seminars on theology and its relationship to daily life. It is attended by over 100,000 people and attracts vast numbers of young people. Any young person in West Germany has the right to a week off school to attend the Kirchentag.

Any legitimate church group can set up a display or exhibition to promote its understanding of the faith. In 1985 a Dutch couple set up an open air exhibition of wood carvings. About twenty in number they each portrayed a different aspect of the nature and ministry of Jesus Christ.

One showed him in crucified form but the wood was old and split down the middle. It was called 'the broken Christ', and speaking of the divided Church, made its own pointed ecumenical confession. Another had been carved out of cheap wood, of a kind that can be bought off the peg from any DIY shop. The wood was a poor specimen, bare and knotted. Any carpenter would have rejected it. It was 'Jesus the poor man'.

A third carving depicted a Christ-figure arising out of and towering above a book. The caption read, 'Jesus is greater than the Bible'. In another, it was only as you looked most carefully that the wood represented a figure at all. It was 'the anonymous Jesus'. 'He comes to us as one unknown', as Albert Schweitzer said. No single carving said everything about Jesus, all of them said something important.

In the course of this chapter we may be able to add another carving to the collection.

> Imagine you are the wood carver. What images would you create to suggest your varied understanding of the nature and work of Jesus Christ?

The idea behind this study book is that it is possible to hear echoes of early Church debate in the pages of the gospels as well as in the letters of Paul and the Acts of the Apostles. The subject for debate we can hear in the Bible passage we are to look at in this chapter is one that rings out loud and clear elsewhere in the New Testament. It rampages through the Acts of the Apostles and Paul's letters so we should not be surprised to hear it in the gospels.

Both Matthew and Mark offer us a story about a woman whose daughter was ill. The story exposes an early Church discussion about the nature of the Church.

'Who can join us?', is the subject. 'Who can belong to the Church?' That is a general question at every point in the history of the Church. The specific question in the early days of the Church was whether Gentiles could join the Church.

How might the early Christian community have developed? It could have become a small Jewish sect paralleling, for example the Essenes, a pietistic group from which many Christians were in fact drawn. As such a group the Christian community would have honoured Jesus as the supreme prophet and studied his teaching.

Alternatively, and still contained within Judaism, it might have become a radical ginger group trying to transform worldwide Judaism and thus been comparable with the Sadducees and Pharisees but making a distinctive Jesus-contribution to the life of Judaism.

But was it enough to remain as a reforming group within Judaism or was more expected of the first Christians if they were to be obedient to their experience of Jesus? Had they in fact met a unique man, offering a unique faith which was bigger than Judaism could contain and so required the creation of a totally new group, in fact a universal Church. Upon that answer hung the whole future of the faith. Had the early Christians reached either of the first two decisions there would be no Church as we now know it, and probably the name of Jesus would long since have dropped out of human history.

The decision that the coming of Jesus had created a new religion and a universal Church was wrung out of hard and painful experience. Paul debated the issue with the Jews at Antioch and said:

**It was necessary that the word of God should be declared to you first. But since you reject it and thus condemn yourselves as unworthy of eternal life, we now turn to the Gentiles. These are our instructions from the Lord.**

*Acts 13.46*

Paul chides Peter:

**When Peter came to Antioch, I opposed him to his face, because he was clearly in the wrong. For until certain persons came from James he was taking his meals with gentile Christians but when they came, he drew back.**

*Galatians 2.11*

This was the same Peter who at some stage in his life, through an experience expressed in the Acts of the Apostles *(Acts 11.1-17)* as a dream was told to accept the unacceptable and forbidden food. It obliged him to wrestle with the nature of the Church and came to the same conclusion that Paul had already reached namely that the formerly unacceptable Gentiles were to be accepted:

**God gave the Gentiles no less a gift than he gave us when we put our trust in the Lord Jesus Christ; then how could I possibly stand in God's way.** *Acts 11.17*

> At some point in his life Peter appears radically to have changed his views about Gentiles in the Church. Invite members of the group to share any significant changes in their own understanding of the Church or the faith over the years of their discipleship.

We can hear this debate in many places in the Gospels. By the time we get to John's gospel *(John 12.20-26)* the issue appears decided. Greeks come to see Jesus. There is a little indecision as Philip consults Andrew before they both go to see whether Jesus will receive the alien visitors but the response of Jesus is unequivocal. In fact their arrival becomes a trigger for John's Jesus to declare that the hour has now come for the Son of Man to be glorified. He is ready to be the solitary grain of wheat to fall into the ground and die, for a rich and universal harvest. The entry of the Gentiles into the Church has become the fulfilment of Judaism.

Similar clear conviction is seen in the synoptic gospels so that Matthew - significantly Matthew, since he is the Jew addressing a Jewish readership - gives Gentile astrologers a place in his opening chapters, alongside the manger bed. *(Matthew 2.1-18).* That too, is a parable of inclusion rather than exclusion.

There is also the story of the eleventh hour workers in which men taken on for the last hour of the day received the same wages as men who had worked throughout the heat and burden of the day. That is not a story about first century industrial relationships but about how Jews who had kept the faith through the heat and burden of imprisonment in Egypt, the struggle in Canaan, exile in Babylon, and so many other deprivations should now open up their new Christian faith-community to Gentiles who had entered only a short time before the now quickly expected end of the world.

Read Matthew 20.1-16 and discuss it in the light of this understanding of the parable.

Elsewhere in the gospels there seems less certainty about letting Gentiles into the Christian community; other strands in the debate are heard. James and John are represented as willing to call down fire from heaven on a Samaritan village, though it is not clear how far its Samaritan-ness was critical. *(Luke 9.51-56)* And clearly there was an ongoing discussion about whether 'not being against us' was as good as 'being for us'.

'Who can join us?', is a wider question than whether Gentiles can enter the Church. Luke seems ever concerned to give a sympathetic push so as to open the door of the Church as wide as possible.

He records Jesus telling a story commending the actions of an old Jewish enemy - the Good Samaritan story. To the story of the one leper who returned to give thanks there is the telling punchline - that he was a Samaritan.

In addition, Luke emphasises incidents in the life of Jesus that draw other people from the margins of life into its centre. For example, he portrays Jesus showing a new and unexpected respect for women. He identifies children as citizens of the Kingdom. Jesus in fact argues that adults must become children before they can be part of that Kingdom of which the Church is a reflection *(Luke 18. 15-7)*. In the Acts of the Apostles he records the baptism of an Ethiopian eunuch, that is the admission into the Church of a man with the double disqualification of being a Gentile and having a physical condition which in Old Testament law would have barred his entrance into most Jewish societies *(Acts 8.26-38)*.

> Which groups of people are marginalised in the Church today?

In all these instances we see the early Church wrestling to know what kind of a community they were to be. What were the conditions of entry? Could anyone be excluded? Slowly, and often painfully the door was opened wider and wider.

That's the trouble with the Gospel! It opens the door to let one deprived group in - Gentiles - only to find all the rest of the marginalised people: women, children, handicapped people, AIDS victims, and homosexuals clamouring to follow.

> Discuss the principle involved. Should we in fact close the door of the Church to any group of people? Do we close the door without intending to?

The story of the Canaanite woman (Mark identifies her as a Gentile, a Phoenician of Syria) whose daughter was ill becomes a window through which we can see the struggle of the early Cristians to understand the nature of their new community.

The story first appeared in Mark's gospel and was later adapted by Matthew. In the account there are strong echoes of the debate about who could join the Church. Further some of the ambivalence we clearly note in the Acts of the Apostles and the Letters of Paul about Gentiles in the Church is also evident. The gospel writers are using the story as a piece of propaganda to try to persuade those who doubt that the admission of Gentiles into the Church has its roots in the ministry and attitudes of Jesus.

### Matthew 15.21-28

21 Jesus then left that place and withdrew to the regions of Tyre and Sidon. 22 And a Canaanite woman from those parts came crying out, 'Sir! have pity on me, Son of David; my daughter is tormented by a devil.' 23 But he said not a word in reply. His disciples came and urged him: 'Send her away; see how she comes shouting after us.' 24 Jesus replied, 'I was sent to the lost sheep of the house of Israel, and to them alone.' 25 But the woman came and fell at his feet and cried, 'Help me, sir.' 26 To this Jesus replied, 'It is not right to take the children's bread and throw it to the dogs.' 27 'True, sir,' she answered; 'and yet the dogs eat the scraps that fall from their master's table.' 28

### Mark 7.24-30

24 Then he left that place and went away into the territory of Tyre. He found a house to stay in and would have liked to remain unrecognised but this was impossible. 25 Almost at once a woman whose young daughter was possessed by an unclean spirit heard of him, came in, and fell at his feet. (She was a Gentile, a Phoenician of Syria by nationality.) 26 She begged him to drive the spirit out of her daughter. 27 He said to her 'Let the children be satisfied first; it is not fair to take the children's bread and throw it to the dogs.' 28 'Sir,' she answered, 'even the dogs under the table eat the children's scraps.' 29 He said to her, 'For saying that you may go home content; the unclean spirit

**Hearing this Jesus replied, 'Woman what faith you have! Be it as you wish!' And from that moment her daughter was restored to health.** *Matthew 16.21-28*

**has gone out of your daughter.' 30 And when she returned home, she found the child lying in bed; the spirit had left her.** *Mark 7.24-30*

Note the way the response develops, and the differences between Matthew and Mark as this Gentile woman approaches Jesus pleading for the healing of her daughter.

| | Matthew | Mark | Response shown |
|---|---|---|---|
| Stage 1: | verse 23 | No record | Jesus is silent but the disciples are in no doubt. 'Get rid of her!' |
| Stage 2: | verse 24 | No record | Jesus now speaks and appears to agree with the disciples. His ministry is to the lost sheep of Israel only. |
| Stage 3: | verse 25 | verse 26 | A fresh, more direct appeal. Both gospel writers are now involved. |
| Stage 4: | verse 26 | verse 27 | Fresh refusal from Jesus on the grounds that he is called to the Jewish children of Israel, not to Gentile dogs. |
| Stage 5: | verse 27 | verse 28 | An apt and winsome reply from the woman about dogs eating scraps from the table. |
| Stage 6: | verse 28 | verse 29 | An apparent change of heart by Jesus, and the healing. |

Mark's account of the incident, written earlier than Matthew's is more relaxed. The women is less demanding. The disciples play no part in the conversation. Jesus' eventual willingness to heal the woman is at first hearing almost quixotic; a reward for clever repartee, though once we realise that 'dogs' was the usual epithet many Jews gave to Gentiles we begin to see that, for Mark too, the story carries implications about the Gentiles' role in the Kingdom of which the children of Israel were the first to hear.

But time has passed before Matthew relates the story. The incident is more intense. The Gentile women knocks on the door twice and far more insistently. The disciples, forerunners of the community of the Church, are drawn into the debate and are dismissive of the foreign woman. Is Matthew using them almost as an Aunt Sally in order to set up the opposition-to-Gentiles-in-the-Church party which, by the end of the story, he is going to knock down?

And the reason for the cure when it comes has far more substance to it. She is favoured, not for a pretty answer with theological overtones of inclusion, but for her faith; that very gift which the Church insisted should be the authenticating evidence - in Jew and Gentile alike - for membership of the Church. Matthew is asserting that the gift of faith is the hallmark of belonging, not nationality or race.

That becomes the answer to the question, 'Who can join the Church?' Those with faith can. There still remain many questions to be answered about the nature of the faith that binds the Church in unity but the essential point has been made: race and nationality are no longer the conditions; faith is the criterion of belonging.

> What are the marks of the faith which is the condition of Church membership? What evidence of it do you look for in those who seek membership of your local church?

A serious question to ask, as we read this narrative is: Where is this debate taking place? It is possible to detect at least two possible locations, though we do not have to choose between them; the same debate can take place in more than one place.

The first possible location we approach with sensitivity. Is this debate taking place within the mind of Jesus himself? Have the gospel-writers captured a moment in his life - parallel to the experiences symbolised by the Temptations, and later by Gethsemane - when Jesus was himself wrestling to understand the nature of his own ministry and the community he was creating?

Did this woman nurture or even plant the seed in the mind of Jesus, that one implication of his message was that he would outgrow Judaism? Was this the day it dawned on Jesus that his message was bigger than he had thought?

Did this Gentile woman in some way change Jesus' mind and become a catalyst in his personal development? Was she to Jesus, what the sheet let down from heaven with foul beasts in it, was to Peter later on? We can only ask the questions but we are obliged to wonder when it first dawned on Jesus that his Gospel was too big for one nation, and whether this was one of several such moments. After all the story begins with Jesus saying 'No', and ends with him saying 'Yes'. That assumes change. In this context it suggests growth and development and poses important Christological questions.

> Is it legitimate to suggest that Jesus had to grow in understanding his own message? If not, why not? If so, identify the points in the life of Jesus where you can discern his growth.

Could we go back to the Dutch couple at the Kirchentag and ask for a carving of 'Jesus the Learner' to be put not only against the young man who at twelve years of age asked perceptive questions in the temple but also at later stages in his life where we too readily think of all his teaching as neatly catalogued and finalised for our unquestioning acceptance? Is there more of the learner in Jesus than there is of the dogmatic theologian offering answers? Here is an account not only of the spiritual growth of the disciples but also of the personal and spiritual growth of Jesus triggered by contact with a foreigner.

If one possible location for this debate is the mind of Jesus himself the second possible location is the one we are exploring in each chapter of this study book. The incident exposes early Church discussion.

During the life of Jesus the twelve disciples found it difficult to think of the activity of God, and certainly of messianic expectations, except in terms of Judaism. Jesus had initially to work within their narrow expectations, exercise his ministry and offer his teaching within the accepted mythology and constraints of the chosen time. Incarnation inevitably imposes constraints. Jesus had to begin his task within what the disciples could conceive before he began to stretch their conceptions.

That, of course, explains why he selected only men as disciples. Because of the role of women in first century society neither the Twelve nor their contemporaries could conceive of women disciples. We must bear that in mind when some parts of the Church deny ordination to women on the grounds that there were no women among the apostles. Similarly, no Roman citizens were called as apostles since that would have been equally inconceivable to those to whom Jesus first spoke. In the twentieth century, the Gospel having taken root in a more developed and less prejudiced society, to prevent women from being ordained on the grounds that Jesus didn't choose any women disciples is as foolish as to preclude the ordination of twentieth century Italians on the grounds that Jesus chose no Romans as his disciples. Or, as the Bishop of Newark, U.S.A., John Shelby Spong, trenchantly asked Dr. Graham Leonard, Bishop of London:

All the disciples of Jesus were Jews. Can only Jews, therefore, be priests? Jesus chose no Polish male. Does that mean that John Paul II is invalidly ordained?

The argument with those who oppose the ordination of women on such grounds is not that they misunderstand women, or ordination, or vocation, but that they seriously misunderstand the implications of incarnation.

If it is a lively issue in your church share your convictions about the ordination of women.

Back to the incident. Does it, therefore, reflect a debate in the mind of Jesus, in the group of disciples and those who came later, about conditions for belonging to the Church?

Take Matthew's account and see Jesus faced with the Gentile question as represented by this woman. It reflects with some accuracy the very stages the early Church later went through, from downright rejection of the Gentiles to final acceptance.

First *(verse 23)* Jesus is silent, just as in the very early days the Church was silent because the issue had not presented itself. Jesus the Jewish Messiah had come to the Jewish people with a new Jewish message.

Then, *(verse 24)*, that view being challenged, he affirms a limited mission - he has come only to the lost sheep of Israel. He is a missionary to revitalise Judaism and challenge its lapsed members just as all the prophets had done before him.

Then comes the struggle *(verses 26-27)* towards a new and universal faith: Who really belongs in this family? - only the children of Israel, or can the Gentile dogs under the table be included?

Finally *(verse 28)* comes the resolution: a 'dog' with faith is a member of the Christian family. Former outcasts are to be accepted; the rejected included.

Matthew has formulated the story in such a way as to present a piece of powerful propaganda aimed at persuading reluctant Jewish Christians to accept Gentiles into the Church. In doing so he has given a careful history of the pilgrimage he and his friends have travelled from early rejection to later acceptance of Gentiles into the Church. In this contribution to the raging argument about whether the Christian community was a Jewish sect or a new religion, Matthew gives the answer that the Church is a new and universal community which has the power to embrace the whole of humanity. What he has already expressed in parable form by inviting foreign visitors to the manger, he now hangs on a specific incident in the life of Jesus. What we see as narrative in the Book of Acts, as philosophical argument in the Letters of Paul, becomes a story in the gospel narrative.

The debate is not yet over. Are we quite sure ourselves who is allowed to be a member of the Christian community? That is a question for the next section of this chapter.

## Chapter Three continued

# The wider debate:
# Who can join the Church?

In the first part of this chapter we overheard the debate in the early Church as the first Christians wrestled with the nature of the new Christian community. Was it to be a reforming Jewish sect or a new religion which broke out of its Jewish origins and welcomed Gentiles into its life? The debate continues for us.

It is heard not on the narrow ground of 'Can Gentiles join the Church?' but on the wider ground of how accepting and inclusive a church can be at local and other levels. Resolution of the question must be as searching, and could be as painful, for us as for the early Jewish Christians considering the admission of Gentiles.

This study can only suggest some possible areas that need to be considered. As groups use the book they will find other topical examples.

It is possible to walk into many British churches today and, in areas of mixed colour and ethnic origin find only white people. Can that be right? Similarly, with a universal gospel and Church can we justify local churches peopled almost exclusively by black members? The contemporary debate must include questions about why the worship and life-style of many of our predominantly 'white churches' alienate black people and why the worship of 'black churches' has less appeal for white people. Is there a black perception of the gospel which is different from the white perception? Is it a cultural difference which also shows itself in entertainment, sport, and leisure pursuits? Should Christianity be able to leap over such cultural differences? Is there in fact a deep-seated racialism in the life of the British Church, fostered by black and white alike, which keeps the two groups of people away from each other in worship? What can we learn from those churches where it is possible to see black and white worshipping together in unity?

The previous paragraph is deliberately expressed in a series of questions because no one study group will be in the same situation or share the same experience as another. Questions rather than dogmatic assertions are our way forward.

The debate about whether the Church is exclusive or inclusive may also challenge us about young people.

Recently, two young people walked into a church during the course of worship. It was in fact a private service rather than a public act of worship and so they were unexpected. Their dress was casual and stood in marked contrast to the formal clothes being worn by the rest of the congregation. The minister records that three things immediately happened to him. He felt spontaneous delight at seeing two unexpected young people in church. He found his language changing to accommodate their presence, and he also glanced instinctively to check the security of a collecting box in the corner! He later wrote: 'God must judge the appropriateness of my spontaneous triple response as I reflect on who we allow to belong to the Christian community.'

Similarly a young convert told of the first day she walked into a church. The church was large and virtually empty with only a scattered congregation. Surrounded by empty pews she sat down in a seat chosen at random. Two minutes before the service started she heard footsteps behind her as another worshipper entered the church. Then a hand tapped her shoulder. 'Excuse me', said a voice, 'you are sitting in my pew.' It says something about the resilience of faith that she is now a member of the Christian Church - though not in the first church she visited!

We should think about children in the context of this study. Of course, we welcome children into the life of the Church. Jesus' comments about millstones round our necks would haunt us forever if we forbade children. But how wide is the door through which we allow children to come? We can slam the door in children's faces without realising it. An eight-year-old was posing questions about community and not simply facial expressions when she said,

*I looked round the church today - why does everyone look so sad? Why can't we have time to get to know each other?*

Similarly, the door for children may be wide enough to let them in as learners but is it wide enough to welcome them as teachers? We won't do what the synagogue in the days of Jesus would have done and direct them to the gallery but we often build a child-size wall around the Communion table.

On what grounds do churches preclude children from Communion? If it is because they do not 'understand' then few adults should be allowed to the Lord's Supper. It cannot be because we doubt their faith since children often have a faith-perception deeper than adults. If it is because they may misinterpret the language of 'flesh, blood, and body' then we should ask how many adults also mis-interpret the language we use. In fact we seem to have developed a pattern which excludes children although it has little relationship to reason or deliberate decision.

Again, we often speak of children as 'tomorrow's church'. Of course, we trust that children, who in the process of growth reach adult life, will in fact be serving the church when those of us who are older have died but if our 'tomorrow's church' label means that we have relegated children to the future and failed to welcome them as true members of the church in the present moment, then they will intuitively recognise that we have excluded them. Little wonder that they then leave us.

The group that wrote the British Council of Churches' report *Child in the Church* share in the debate as they affirm:

*Children are a gift to the Church. The Lord of the Church sets them in the midst of the Church, today as in Galilee, not as objects of benevolence, nor even as recipients of instruction, but in the last analysis as patterns of discipleship. The Church that does not accept children unconditionally into its fellowship is depriving those children of what is rightfully theirs, but the deprivation such a Church will itself suffer is far more grave.*

'Who may belong to the Church?' can be seen acutely in whom we allow to receive Communion? It is interesting to listen to the varied invitations to Communion given in the Free Churches. The boundaries are clearly set and the patterns of inclusion and exclusion defined.

Sometimes it is for 'those who love our Lord Jesus Christ and seek to serve him'. Yet the biblical perception is: 'We love because he loved us first' *(1 John 4.19).* His love has priority in the relationship. To make our love for God a condition of receiving his gifts is to reverse the gospel understanding of God's initiative in loving. Sometimes the invitation is to 'members of this and any other branch of the Christian Church'. That is wide but is it wide enough? May not the Communion Service be the occasion in which the beginnings of faith dawn and exclusion from it be a denial of opportunity to the Holy Spirit? Can there be any more reason for excluding people from the Table than for excluding them from a preaching service? Is not being in the church at that moment a sufficient ground for receiving whatever gifts God offers at the Table of his Son?

Some parts of the Christian Church have creeds which form either doors people can enter or barriers that exclude. The historic creeds were hammered out of experience at periods when there was great debate and argument in the Church about its beliefs. They were written as much to define error as to explain truth. Their aim was to show the boundaries of belief and thus decide who was included and who was excluded. For this and other reasons the Free Churches have always been cautious about creeds not least because of their tight definitions. Credal statements fail to recognise that not only do words change their meaning but that Christian thought develops, thus making earlier definitions suspect or even redundant. Instead the Free Churches have made occasional Statements of Faith at critical points in their lives. Such Statements are more open and immediate than creeds and thus less binding on the future. Yet, within a long-term creed or a short-term statement the faith is stated and the boundaries of belief established. Should we insist that newcomers 'sign on the dotted line' if they want to be members or should we adjust our current creed or statement to meet the experience and insights of the new believer? Or do we in fact do both and if so how do we judge what to retain from the past and what to receive from the present?

There is a dilemma to be worked through. The Church needs an identity. It is a group of people with a common belief and recognisable practices. If the door is thrown wide open and no questions asked or demands made on those who seek to join, then its message becomes watered down and ineffective. Yet, with a Lord who strode across barriers and a group of early members who broke the rules tradition had laid down for them, it must always be anxious to keep its doors as wide open as possible. A.E.Harvey is thinking of the Church of England when he shares in this debate and outlines part of the dilemma in his book *'Believing and*

*Belonging'.* His comments are relevant to all the churches.
*How open and welcoming can a church afford to be? Can it really accept anyone as a member so long as he or she is an honest enquirer, ready to suspend judgment on a number of important matters until the mysterious ethos of the Church of England gradually seeps into heart and mind? Is there not a danger that it may lose hold of vital truths unless it proclaims clearly the doctrines which must be accepted by every member? This certainly was the motive of the great revivals of the eighteenth and nineteenth centuries . . .*

*It seemed and still seems to many church-people that there are certain Christian truths which must be held on to, come what may, and that no-one can be accepted in the family of the church who has serious doubts about them . . .*

*And yet this apparently sensible view of the church collides with the awkward fact that you cannot actually* **compel** *people to believe anything. What an individual does or does not believe is a highly personal matter . . .*

*The result of all this, of course is tension. Just as a trade union or a political party requires absolute solidarity from its members if it is going to achieve its ends, and yet must encourage new ideas and differences of opinion if it is to remain a living force, so the church, like any other institution, requires its members to stand together against the attacks and challenges of the secular world, and yet at the same time must encourage discussion, debate, and new thinking in the interpretation of its historic teaching and in the application of the Christian gospel to the modern world.*

'Who belongs?' is still our question, long after unexpected aliens knelt at the manger, and Jesus broke the then recognised rules for a person from Canaan with the double handicap of being a woman and a foreigner. In that story Matthew clarified the issue: race can be ignored; faith is the new criterion for belonging. He sets this conviction in a story which gives his assertion the authority of Jesus.

We wrestle with comparable questions in different contexts. Can we say: Age can be ignored; faith is the new criterion for belonging? Can sexual orientation be ignored where there is faith? How far can we ignore theological differences or different interpretations of the Gospel? Perhaps those who accept the story of the Virgin birth as literal can live alongside those who see the story as a parable but how far can Christians who have widely varying beliefs about the resurrection of Jesus live together? Are we to say that doctrine can be ignored because faith is the new criterion for belonging?

'I don't believe in a life after death' a Church Secretary confided in a minister when he preached at a church as a visitor. Should he have written to the church to question whether it was right for the Secretary to remain a leader in the community whilst holding a view which runs counter to basic Christian affirmations, or rejoice that the church was able to hold an honest searcher not only within its fellowship but as a leader? Rabbi Hugo Gryn has said that religions today are divided into those which have all the questions and those which have all the answers - but the trouble is that the answers do not match the questions. Those who are more aware of the questions are less likely to be able to make formal affirmations of belief. Can the Church receive them with the same warmth as it receives those who can accept the traditional answers?

Life-style raises the same kind of questions. There are few congregations without a number of divorced members. In welcoming them are we exhibiting Christian acceptance or merely conforming to the passing morality of our secular times? How does a congregation re-act when it sees the marriage of two of its members dissolving before its eyes? A few decades ago the couple would quietly have disappeared from the congregation, a few centuries ago they would probably have been driven out. In arguing that in such circumstances 'it is not for us to judge' are we displaying Christian acceptance or neglecting our moral duty?

If there is a choice to be made between the risk of excluding people because they do not conform to the accepted norms of belief and behaviour in the Church, and the risk of including people who may be inappropriate members of the Church, the evidence of biblical experience and the life of Jesus points to our taking the latter risk and opening the doors wide.

**For group discussion**

1 A church in the north of England is set in a pre-dominantly Asian community. The majority of the church members, who used to live in the immediate vicinity of the church but over the years have moved to other parts of the town, now travel several miles into the church each Sunday to a congregation that is exclusively white. What questions would you want to put to this church?

2 What contribution can young people make to the life of a church and in what way is it different from the contribution of older people?

3 Think of any people who have started coming to your church in recent years. What have they contributed to your church life? In what ways has the church changed because of their coming?

4 Invite a recent visitor or new member to share with you his/her first impressions of your church.

5 A bishop has a declared policy of being willing to confirm homosexuals and welcome them into the churches of his diocese but refuses to ordain homosexuals as priests. Is this a consistent policy?

6 'To call children "tomorrow's church" is to ignore the resources children bring into the church of today'. Discuss this and identify the resources which children offer to a church.

7 Should each church clearly set out its beliefs, practices, and moral requirements in detail and oblige every potential member to subscribe to them before accepting them into membership?

## Chapter Four

# The gospel stories: Doubting Thomas and The journey to Emmaus

In the final chapter we turn to other passages from the Bible which provide us with windows through which we can see the agenda of the early Church and share in another early Christian debate. Before we do so it may be helpful to say a little more about the different kinds of debate and discussion we have been considering.

The story of the epileptic boy exposed the agenda item, 'Why with all the resources of God do Christians sometimes fail?' It was possible to draw out three distinct elements in the debate:

- we fail because we don't pray enough
- we fail because we don't fast enough
- we fail because we haven't enough faith.

The three elements were not necessarily contradictory. They are certainly not exhaustive. There is no suggestion that the existence of three answers proved to be divisive in the church communities. They represented different attitudes to a common problem and, since they appear as individual comments in different gospels, it is likely that one or the other of these explanations of failure attracted a particular local church community. One could imagine three people in one room discussing the question or three Christian groups, one in say Antioch, one in Jerusalem, and a third in Rome facing up to the same question but getting different answers. Thus each of the gospel writers, relating to one of the answers, let it influence the way he told the story.

The 'coin in the fish's mouth' story gave us the agenda item, 'How does the Christian community respond to earthly authorities?' The story only appeared in Matthew's gospel so the varying voices in the debate had to be disentangled from one account. The voices weren't as well defined as in the story of the epileptic boy. That second debate sounded more like an ongoing and changing discussion, perhaps with the same people getting different answers at different times.

The story of the Canaanite woman was different again. The early church agenda item was identified as being, 'Who can join the Church?', and arising from the agonies the Church faced about the admission of Gentiles. We know from elsewhere in the New Testament that this was an issue which tragically divided the early Church and on its outcome depended whether the Christian community would become a distinctive Jewish sect or a universal Church. We saw the story as one of Matthew's several elaborate and precise story-arguments to support the admission of Gentiles into the Church, and that just as he had created the parable of the manger-visiting Gentile astrologers to promote his view of Christianity as a universal faith, so he hung the same argument and appeal on this incident when Jesus welcomed a Gentile woman. But again, it is a different type of contribution to a debate; a precisely fashioned, almost manicured, contribution.

In this final chapter we examine several stories describing resurrection appearances, and in particular the story of the appearance of Jesus to two travellers on the road to Emmaus. What style of debate does this passage reveal? We shall find no animosity or anger in the debate. It is the kind of discussion in which there may be differences of opinion but the opinions hang together, all of a piece. It is not wrangling argument but a discussion in which mutual friends explore an agreed truth together.

The agenda item is, 'How do we authenticate the resurrection appearances of Jesus?' It may even be wider than that. There is a complex of arguments around our chosen passage. It may be touching on another agenda item namely, 'In the light of his death and resurrection how do we authenticate the total Jesus experience?' The questions will reveal themselves as we proceed. We shall eventually get to the Emmaus road story but we have a sabbath day's journey to travel before we can consider it.

We begin outside the synoptic gospels and with the final verse of John's gospel. During the course of his gospel he has told us a good deal about Jesus but he finally adds:

**There is much else that Jesus did. If it were all to be recorded in detail, I suppose the whole world could not hold the books that would be written.**          *John 21.25*

It parallels what he had written at the end of the previous chapter:

**There were indeed many other signs that Jesus performed in the presence of his disciples, which are not recorded in this book. Those here written have been recorded in order that you may hold the faith that Jesus is the Christ, the Son of God and that through this faith you may possess life by his name.**          *John 20.30-31*

> From your knowledge of the gospels written by Matthew, Luke, and Mark suggest what sentence they would have written to show their motive in writing the gospel apart, of course, from the essential motive of spreading the Gospel.

Paul corroborates John's information *(1 Corinthians 15.3-7)* when he gives examples of resurrection appearances - on one occasion to five hundred people - which is not recorded in the gospel accounts. The gospels simply do not, because they cannot, tell us all that happened to Jesus and his disciples. John tells us his motivation in choosing what to put in and what to keep out; he has chosen those stories which will promote the faith that Jesus is the Christ, the Son of God. Presumably the other gospel writers had their own motivation and priorities.

So we learn three things:

1. that there were many more stories about Jesus the gospel writers could have told us and more resurrection appearances than those recorded in the four gospels.
2. that, therefore, each gospel writer was selective and had to be.
3. that under the broad banner of proclaiming the good news, variations of motive in selecting the stories in each gospel is to be expected.

A.E. Harvey writes:

*The conviction that Jesus had 'risen from the dead' was not reached at the same time and in the same way by all the disciples, and many different stories about these critical days must have been current. Each evangelist will have chosen to narrate the particular experience which seemed to bring out most clearly for him the meaning of this almost unimaginable event.*

Look at some of the stories and assess the possible motivation behind them. First, the Thomas story:

**Late that Sunday evening, when the disciples were together behind locked doors, for fear of the Jews, Jesus came and stood among them. 'Peace be with you!' he said, and then showed them his hands and his side. So when the disciples saw the Lord, they were filled with joy. Jesus repeated, 'Peace be with you!', and said, 'As the Father sent me, so I send you.' Then he breathed on them, saying, 'Receive the Holy Spirit!' If you forgive any man's sins, they stand forgiven; if you pronounce them unforgiven, unforgiven**

they remain.'

One of the Twelve, Thomas, that is 'the Twin', was not with the rest when Jesus came. So the disciples told him, 'We have seen the Lord.' He said, 'Unless I see the mark of the nails on his hands, unless I put my finger into the place where the nails were, and my hand into his side, I will not believe it.'

A week later his disciples were again in the room, and Thomas was with them. Although the doors were locked, Jesus came and stood among them, saying, 'Peace be with you!' Then he said to Thomas, 'Reach your finger here; see my hands. Reach your hand here and put it into my side. Be unbelieving no longer, but believe.' Thomas said, 'My Lord and my God!' Jesus said, 'because you have seen me you have found faith. Happy are they who never saw me and yet have found faith.'                      *John 20.19-29.*

The story refers to events on Easter evening but was obviously written up with much later issues in mind. Jesus appears to the disciples. He shows his hands and side to identify himself. They can now say, 'We have seen the Lord.' But Thomas, not being present, wants the same corroborating evidence. Only sight and touch will satisfy him.

The following Sunday Thomas experiences the risen Lord in the same way. He makes his confession of faith. All is well and the incident is neatly completed. But John gives Jesus a critically important punch line which reveals a major reason for telling the story for posterity: 'Because you have seen me, you have found faith; happy are they who never saw me, yet found faith.'

Amongst all the possible stories to tell, why did John include this one? First, because it establishes the fact that the first disciples did 'see Jesus' on Easter evening. Thus, it offers an argument to critics who said that belief in the resurrection was hearsay and not founded on personal experience.

There is a second motive. Thirty years on from the first Easter the original disciples were getting older. There were many new converts in the Church including Gentiles who were not involved in early days and had not seen Jesus by the Sea of Galilee teaching the crowds, nor watched him ride into Jerusalem on a donkey, nor seen him die on Calvary. Certainly they had not stood with Mary by the garden tomb, nor eaten a meal with the risen Christ on the beach. They were second-generation Christians. With the first generation of Christians dying off it had to be made clear by the Church that the faith of the second generation was as valid and authentic as the faith of Peter, James and John. For long years the new Christians had been able to lean on the faith of the first Christians. But what would happen when they died?

> Imagine yourself to be in the second generation after Christ and attracted to the Church. What questions would you feel it necessary to ask the original disciples before seeking to join the Christian community?

The Thomas story is part of the early Church's attempt to make sure that its life could continue into the time when none of the Twelve were alive. The story pictures Jesus saying to the Twelve, that is to the original people who knew him 'in the flesh', 'Because you have seen me you have found faith'. Then the story turns its attention to Thomas, representing those who had not seen Jesus - that is believers of the second, third, fourth generation and beyond into the twentieth century. Their faith is authenticated as strongly as was the faith of the first believers: 'though you never saw me, you found faith.' John makes his point that faith is all that matters whether it comes from sight or not-sight. Thus, the means of authenticating Christian experience, moves from 'seeing Jesus' to 'faith in Jesus'. The Church receives authority to march into future generations. Thus one motive for including the story is to prepare for the future. The seven days between the two Sundays has become a symbol for a generation.

Recall the beach resurrection scene in John's gospel *(John 21)* where the disciples are in the boat and Jesus calls them, and then guides them in their fishing. Peter leaps out of the boat and swims to land. A thrice repeated question is asked: 'Do you love me?', and Peter's triple affirming response follows. Then Peter asks about John:

**'Lord, what will happen to him?' Jesus said, 'If it should be my will that he wait until I come, what is it to you? Follow me?**

It is an ambiguous response.

> Decide and discuss the various possible meanings to Jesus' comment about John.

These words of Jesus were remembered by some Christians and used as an argument that the return of Jesus would be soon, and before John died. Such a belief would have influenced the entire pattern of church-life and Christian behaviour. To John, writing his gospel and fast approaching old age, it is becoming clear that they have got it wrong. Jesus isn't returning yet. So one of several motives for writing this story is to try to change the tradition. The tradition had been: Jesus will be back before John dies. What damage it would have done to the integrity of the Church if they had told that story to unbelievers, and what confusion it would have caused within the Church when John died and Jesus had not returned.

But the original saying is ambiguous so John writes his story in such a way as to switch the interpretation to the other side of the ambiguity and thus take account of the probability of his own death before the return of Jesus. Therefore, he writes:

**That saying of Jesus became current in the brotherhood, and was taken to mean that that disciple would not die. But in fact Jesus did not say that he would not die; he only said, 'If it should be my will that he wait until I come, what is it to you?'** *John 21.23*

This chapter has gone a long way round to reach the beginning of the journey to Emmaus. It has done so to establish some clear principles. Using evidence from John's gospel and Paul's first letter to the Corinthians we have seen that throughout the gospels, and certainly with the resurrection stories, we can discern primary and secondary motives for including one story rather than another. All the resurrection stories have the primary motive of bringing us to faith but many also have secondary motives which, if we can discover them, shed fascinating light on the early Church and its internal discussions. Early Church agenda items lie within the accounts and we have seen some of the items, for example:

Can resurrection actually happen and if so, what sort of a post-resurrection body is involved?

Is the faith of those who never actually saw Jesus as valid as those who lived with him for three years and were witnesses to the whole experience?

What explanation can be offered for the apparent error of our earlier belief, founded on accredited words of Jesus, that he would return within John's lifetime?

The resurrection stories are particularly important as windows through which we see the early Church agenda because by their very nature and the event they are documenting they are tentative and searching. You can't pin them down in the way that you can isolate and identify the story of Zaccheus up a tree, or a parable of a Samaritan who unexpectedly turned out to be good.

How does this help us in understanding the Emmaus resurrection story?

That same day two of them were on their way to a village called Emmaus, which lay about seven miles from Jerusalem, and they were talking together about all these happenings. As they talked and discussed it with one another, Jesus himself came up and walked along with them; but something kept them from seeing who it was. He asked them, 'What is it you are debating as you walk?' They halted, their faces full of gloom, and one, called Cleopas, answered, 'Are you the only person staying in Jerusalem not to know what has happened there in the last few days?' 'What do you mean?' he said. 'All this about Jesus of Nazareth,' they replied, 'a prophet powerful in speech and action before God and the whole people; how our chief priests and rulers handed him over to be sentenced to death, and crucified him. But we had hoped that he was the man to liberate Israel. What is more, this is the third day since it happened, and now some women of our company have astounded us: they went early to the tomb, but failed to find his body, and returned with a story that they had seen a vision of angels who told them he was alive. So some of our people went to the tomb and found things just as the women had said; but him they did not see.'

'How dull you are!' he answered. 'How slow to believe all that the prophets said! Was the Messiah not bound to suffer thus before entering upon his glory?' Then he began with Moses and all the prophets, and explained to them the passages which referred to himself in every part of the scriptures.

By this time they had reached the village to which they were going, and he made as if to continue his journey, but they pressed him: 'Stay with us, for evening draws on, and the day is almost over.' So he went in to stay with them. And when he had sat down with them at table, he took bread and said the blessing; he broke the bread, and offered it to them. Then their eyes were opened, and they recognised him; and he vanished from their sight. They said to one another, 'Did we not feel our hearts on fire as he talked with us on the road and explained the scriptures to us?'

Without a moment's delay they set out and returned to Jerusalem. There they found that the Eleven and the rest of the company had assembled, and were saying, 'It is true: the Lord has risen; he has appeared to Simon.' They gave their account of the events of their journey and told how he had been recognised by them at the breaking of the bread.

*Luke 24.13-35*

The primary motivation of the story remains the same - to convince readers and bring them to faith. But, reading the account, we can identify early Church discussions about resurrection, and disentangle some of the elements of the debate. They are not acrimonious arguments but the kind of discussion in which believers help each other to explore their common belief.

Imagine a discussion around the agenda item, 'How do we authenticate an experience of the resurrection of Jesus?' or 'How do we know when such an experience is real or not?' Here are two people rushing back in the late evening from a fourteen mile round trip and they say: 'We have seen Jesus'. Here is Peter on the beach, Mary in a garden, and on one occasion five hundred people altogether. They all offer stories of resurrection experiences. Do you trust them all? Have they equal validity? Is there the danger of someone making a story up? A single individual can be misled and five hundred people can suffer mass hysteria? What tests do you apply?

When a newcomer seeks membership in your church, how do you decide whether his/her faith is valid and that membership is appropriate? What tests do you apply?

Our problem as we consider such questions is that we now have a completed Bible so we know which stories were accepted but nothing of the stories that were rejected. If only we could see Luke's waste paper basket or the pile of papyrus on John's desk marked 'Rejected'! It would be fascinating to listen in on an early Church discussion about their resurrection experiences and hear the criteria they used as they sought to understand them. All we can do is to try to look underneath the surface of their final choices, of which the Emmaus story is one. The story gives some help in showing how they made their choices, and the nature of their debate.

The first disciples did not come to Christian belief out of a vacuum. They were Jews with Jewish beliefs. In chapter 2 we noted the argument between Pharisees and Sadducees in which the former believed in resurrection and the latter did not. That argument would be well-known to the disciples when, before they knew Jesus, they attended the synagogue and shared in normal Jewish discussion. Each of the disciples had probably lined up behind one of those convictions. Had the Jesus experience changed their ideas? If so, how did they justify the change?

What voices can we hear in the Emmaus account as the early Christians discuss their unprecedented experience of resurrection?

First, 'if resurrection is true it must interlock with our Jewish convictions represented by the Old Testament.' Those Jewish traditions and documents could be adjusted but could not be totally rejected. The words Jesus spoke on the Emmaus Road are part of the process by which their old experience is seen to interlock with their new experience. Moses, the prophets and the Psalms are shown to be unexpected pointers to the life of Jesus. They are called on to justify how the Messiah could be crucified and in so doing they begin the process of understanding resurrection.

It is fair to ask where those words on the lips of Jesus on the Emmaus Road came from even if in the end our lack of knowledge means we cannot give a definitive answer. Were they spoken by Jesus, remembered by the two on the road, and then recorded by Luke? It is not only literalists who would accept that interpretation; many others would see the words originating with Jesus, even if they were later adapted.

Equally, it could be argued that they are the product of the disciples agonising through discussion and debate over the years in the early Church and then written up by Luke. In this sense they might have been an early sermon, comparable to the sermons of Peter and Stephen in the Acts of the Apostles which was also written by Luke.

> Invite any members of the group not brought up in the Church to describe how far they had (1) to reject, or (2) adapt their previous experience of life to their new Christian experience.

Secondly, we cannot fail to notice that the heart of the Emmaus resurrection experience lay at the table, in the meal. That is when they recognised him. Resurrection is here clearly linked with what some of us call Communion - others Eucharist, the Lord's Supper, the Mass, the Breaking of Bread. Jesus, in the Emmaus story turns an ordinary meal into a Communion Service. The guest becomes the host. Is this story selected when others were rejected because it undergirds the importance of the Communion meal? We know too little about the development of Communion in the very early days of the Church. The Acts of the Apostles points to it, so do the Letters of Paul but the precise pattern of development is difficult to chart. But the Emmaus story identifies a link between Communion and resurrection and the hinted argument that resurrection is validated by its intimate connection with the breaking of the bread and the presence of Christ experienced in the Lord's Supper.

> At what points in the life of the Church has your conviction about the resurrection of Christ been confirmed for example, in preaching, hymn-singing, the Communion Service, conversation?
> Is the main thrust of the Communion Service for you a memorial to the sacrificial death of Christ or a proclamation of his risen life?

There is a third voice. It talks not about Communion, but about community. Immediately after the resurrection appearance the two travellers rushed back to the rest of their friends. In doing so they took a risk. The stranger had been pressed to stay at Emmaus for the night because it was getting dark and thus dangerous to proceed. Yet, perhaps an hour or more later and disregarding the danger, they felt compelled to go back to the community.

The community was important for witness. Naturally, they wanted to share their newfound belief and so must tell their friends that Jesus was risen but would it not also be important for them that the other Christians recognised and affirmed their experience? Resurrection was to be seen as integral to the whole Christian community and not a phenomenon which two individuals had experienced. The story closes with the disciples in Jerusalem confirming the experience of the two by speaking of Simon Peter's comparable experience, and is quickly followed by the story of another resurrection appearance which they all experience together as one community of believers.

> Can you talk to other believers about your personal faith? What hinders or helps you? Similarly, what hinders or helps

your conversation with those who do not believe?

Luke appears to be arguing that to validate a personal experience of the resurrection of Jesus it must be possible to see a common thread which binds it to the experience of the total church community. It suggests the process: test your experience by laying it alongside mine as I will test my experience by reference to yours. Although resurrection, like many other spiritual experiences is essentially personal it is not private and must be seen to be part of a corporate experience of the whole community. Was it in this way that the first Christian community sifted out idiosyncratic experiences or notions of resurrection that owed more to the quirks and fancies of individuals than to an encounter with the living Lord of the Church?

This makes our discussion similar to the debate about authority in chapter 2, especially when an individual rebels or disagrees with church authority. The individual rebel within the Church must test his personal ideas against those of friends. Am I a crank or are there others who agree with me? And if there is a good number that agree with me, are we all cranks or is the Church in fact to be questioned and opposed?

Two people had an experience at Emmaus. Was it valid or was it that they were tired after three traumatic days and a long journey and so dreamt it all? After all, the stranger disappeared. Even Cinderella left a glass slipper but this stranger left nothing tangible. As the slipper was tested so must the experience of the two be tested against the experience of the community. The journey back was not only to share good news, it was to see whether a personal experience held credence within the wider community.

'This stranger left nothing tangible.' But what did he leave?

To summarise. We can hear at least three voices in the Emmaus story which participate in the debate about the validity and authentication of resurrection.

Can it be seen as a development of the Jewish tradition which we have learned to trust?

How does it relate to one of the central acts of the Church - the breaking of the bread?

Does the personal experience of resurrection interlock with the corporate experience of the whole community?

We have not heard the whole debate about resurrection. It continues today. In the next section of the chapter we invite contemporary voices to share in the discussion.

*Chapter Four continued*

# The wider debate: Resurrection

No one today can say 'I have seen the Lord' in a physical sense. We cannot stand by the empty tomb and so we have no material evidence that there was one. The evidence for resurrection has to be deduced. How is it deduced?

The two theologian brothers Anthony and Richard Hanson go to the Church as evidence.

*It is probably true to say that nobody well-informed would believe the evidence of the resurrection simply by reading it once. We believe it because we have encountered the risen Christ in the experience of the Church. The evidence for the resurrection provides sufficient historical basis for our faith, but not full proof. When all is said and done, the main evidence for the resurrection as an actual event lies in the faith and behaviour of the earliest disciples. No other explanation seems adequate.*

from *'Reasonable Belief'*

C.H.Dodd also goes to the evidence of the changed lives of the first disciples:

*Clearly **something** had changed these men. They said it was a meeting with Jesus. We have no evidence with which to check their claim. To propose an alternative explanation, based on some preconceived theory, is of dubious profit. What was the nature of this meeting we cannot pretend to know. What actually happened, if by that we mean what* *any casual observer might have witnessed, is a question that does not admit of an answer. But the events that make history do not consist of such 'bare facts.' They include the meaning of the facts held for those who encountered them; and their reality is known through the observable consequences. In this instance we may be clearer about the meaning and the consequences than about the 'facts' in themselves, but this would be true of other momentous events in history. We are dealing with a truly 'historic' event. It was the culmination of previous events in the lives of these men (summed up in their memories of Jesus), and the creative starting point of a new sequence of events of which the world was soon aware. It made them new men, but it was also the birth of a new community. Or rather, as they would have said, it was the rebirth of the people of God, the rising of Israel from the dead and they were in it. It is because they speak out of the very centre of this 'new creation' that their witness carries weight. They themselves had passed through death to new life. The darkness and desolation of Good Friday and the miserable sabbath which followed it had emptied life of all meaning for them. On the 'third day' they were 'raised to life with Christ' as Paul put it; and that is a confession of faith hardly less basic than the proclamation, 'Christ is risen.'*

from *'The Founder of Christianity'*

Fr Harry Williams takes the argument a stage further and brings it into the present day. The resurrection, he contends is not only about what happened to Jesus and his disciples but about what happens to us. More significantly it is not only about some future event and our hopes of a life after death; it is about what happens to us in our own daily, personal experience.

*An artist, at first only painfully aware of utter emptiness and impotence, finds his imagination gradually stirred into life and discovers a vision which takes control of him and which he feels not only able but compelled to express. That is resurrection. Or a scholar or scientist as he pursues his research finds a favourite theory breaking up in his hands. He is left with no home in which to house the quantities of evidence he has collected. Then a new more adequate theory gradually takes shape in his mind which makes him more at home with his material even than he was before. That is resurrection. Or a married couple find their old relationship, once rich and fulfilling, slowly drying up into no more than an external observance to the point where it seems impossible that these dry bones should ever live again. Then a new relationship emerges, less superficially high powered and less greedy than the old one, but deeper, more stable, more satisfying, with a new quality of life which is inexhaustible because it does not depend on the constant recharging of emotional batteries. That is resurrection.* from '*True Resurrection*'

In a similar way Harry Williams continues to identify the resurrection experiences of others. He tells of a man who though outwardly successful is inwardly deprived but who discovers a broader base for his life and so is regenerated. He suggests that as people work through bereavement that, although they are never the same again, out of their suffering they find themselves in touch with a new dimension of reality. He concludes:

*Resurrection is always a mystery. It is always a miracle. It is always the creative act of the Eternal Word. Because that Word is spoken now in the present in terms of what we call the common circumstances of life, there can be nobody who at some time or another has not thus been raised from the dead.*

In his book *A Matter of Life and Death* John V.Taylor tells a story he first heard as a radio talk. The broadcaster had pioneered ameliorative work among the very old. She described a typical institution she had visited. It is a resurrection experience.

*They were all sitting half dead in their wheel chairs, mostly paralysed and just existing, they didn't live. They watched some television, but if you had asked them what they had watched they would probably not have been able to tell you. We brought in a young woman who was a dancer and we told her to play beautiful old-fashioned music. She brought in Tchaikovsky records and so on and started to dance among these old people, all in their wheel-chairs, which had been set in a circle. In no time the old people started to move. One old man stared at his hand and said, 'Oh my God, I haven't moved this hand in ten years.' And the 104-year-old, in a thick German accent, said 'that reminds me of when I danced for the Tsar of Russia.'*

Is it legitimate to take the once-for-all event of the resurrection of Jesus Christ from the dead and compare it with the resurgent feelings of a tired artist, the regeneration of a weary businessman, the recovery of love in a dry marriage, the stirrings of thought and movement in an old people's home, or even our painful rebirth after bereavement? Is it possible to talk in the same breath of the glorious resurrection of Jesus Christ the Son of God and our feeble stirrings without either belittling his amazing victory over death or claiming too much for our own limited experience?

But does such a comparison belittle or does it interpret? Do you belittle the depths of the ocean by paddling in the shallows? Does the overture belittle the opera, or is the fullness of human love belittled by the first adolescent kiss? In fact, the greater gives promise to the lesser and the lesser translates the greater into a form we can understand. It is when resurrection is seen to be experienced and understood in the commonplace that we glimpse its vitality and power in the dramatic events which surrounded Jesus and the birth of the Christian community.

To see how our own experiences reflect and interpret the

glorious resurrection of Jesus Christ means that we are no longer spectators of events that took place two thousand years ago and which we can only see as on a distant stage, but that we are involved in the action ourselves and part of an eternal drama in which every generation plays its part.

And so the debate about resurrection continues and invites us to share not only in the discussion about it but in the very resurrection drama itself.

**For group discussion**

1 What is it about the life and attitudes of the early Christians that corroborates the resurrection of Jesus?

2 C.H.Dodd draws a distinction between the 'meaning and consequences' of what happened to the disciples and the 'facts' of what happened. Is there a similar distinction to be drawn about the Christian life today?

3 Think about Harry Williams' examples of resurrection today: the artists, the scholar, the married couple. After each example he affirms: that is resurrection. What examples from (1) other people's experience and, (2) your own experience can you describe, and say: that is resurrection.

4 What does the word 'resurrection' mean to you now?

5 Given a controversial subject does your study group tend to fight or take flight?

6 What do you do in your church when two members disagree on an important subject?

# Continuing questions

## At least two questions remain.

The first is to ask how far we can still see Jesus within the pages of the gospels. The stories we have studied appear to have been carefully crafted by the gospel writers to reflect and address the theological debate of the early Church. If that was their purpose in substantial sections of the gospel narrative have they thereby obscured the figure of the man about whom they intended to write? In telling us about the Church have they lost Jesus and by our listening so intently to the Church-centred arguments do we fail to hear Jesus himself from the pages of the gospels?

Certainly, we can now see the historical Jesus only through the eyes of the first Christians, and in particular through the edited stories they wrote about him. To pretend to more is to deceive ourselves and put our mission on shaky foundations.

As long ago as 1934, Rudolf Bultmann took a pessimistic view.

*I do indeed think that we can now know almost nothing concerning the life and personality of Jesus.*

Bultmann's pessimism must be balanced by C.H.Dodd's affirmation. Speaking of the four gospels he argues that they are

*... so consistent, so coherent, and withal so distinctive in manner, style, content, that no reasonable critic should doubt ... that we find reflected here the thought of a single unique teacher.*

Those words come from a gifted New Testament scholar. They echo what we instinctively feel as we read the gospel narratives. The life of the early Church may be the context in which Jesus is presented to us but he stands in strong relief against his background so that we see him for himself. Without the reality of his teaching and the dynamism of his life there would have been no need for discussion and, in fact, no community in which the debate could have taken place.

The truth which the gospel writers share with us and which the early Christians reached only 'after much discussion' is Christ himself. His life-style, his obedience to God, and his resurrection make him a free man, bound by no chains. He is free to break out of the first century in which he was born and to span the ages. He meets every generation as its contemporary. That is the faith which prompted the gospel writers to begin their work. Inevitably they speak of him within the context of their own time because that is where they met him but they cannot hold him within their time. As they address the questions which his coming posed for them they thereby provide us with valued resources as we face the questions the same Lord obliges us to ask in our time. Faith unites us with those pioneers of the Church community even more effectively than do the debates in which they originated and we share. It is a faith which derives not from a dead hero but a living Lord.

The second question relates to the nature and value of that Christian debate which has been the underlying theme of this study book. Knowing that discussion and debate is well heard in the Acts of the Apostles and the Letters of Paul we have tried to hear it in the less expected place of the gospels. Debate is important because it is an anvil on which we beat out our beliefs and convictions. That is no less true in our own time than in the time of the early Church.

The Christian Church is not very good at debate. We are either afraid of it or do not know how to use it. In the terms used in group dynamics we fall for the 'fight or flight' syndrome, that is we either let debate destroy us, and sadly Christian history is littered with examples of that, or more commonly in the late twentieth century, we avoid serious debate of controversial issues because we don't know how to cope with serious disagreement.

So, for example, Archbishop Lefebre is excommunicated from the Roman Catholic Church as though there was no common ground between him and the rest of his church on which debate could take place. Similarly, when it comes to the crunch too many church union schemes tend to paper over the cracks of church division rather than face up to them. Most local churches fight shy of political debate because it would be too controversial and painful. In fact, through discussion and debate, we ought to be able to help each other to think through vital issues using disagreement as a resource rather than a weapon.

How many local churches could discuss the nuclear issues creatively? Do Councils of Churches, involving Roman Catholics and Protestants, discuss abortion and contraception? Have the mainstream churches stopped hearing the testimony of Quakers and Salvationists about Holy Communion? Could the women's meeting debate whether homosexuals should be ordained? Can those who worship together share their party political allegiance and discuss their political differences in a Christian forum, or does the danger of a fight mean that we quickly take flight from such suggestions?

The issues vary from time to time; our inability to deal with them in a sustained way and at a serious level remains. We are not skilled at dealing with controversy creatively.

Where there is no vision the people perish. Where there is no debate the vision cannot be shared. Rigorous debate in which the participants had to learn how to cope with deep feelings of anger, frustration and hurt rampages through the pages of the New Testament. It was out of the agony and joy of controversial debate held within the love of Christ that the first Christians formed their faith. We ought not to deny ourselves the joy of such an encounter, and we have no right to expect to be excused the agony.